# CHRIST AND THE SPIRIT

# CHRIST AND THE SPIRIT

The Doctrine of the Incarnation
According to Edward Irving

*By*

**Graham McFarlane**

paternoster press

Copyright © Graham McFarlane 1996

First published 1996
by Paternoster Press, P.O. Box 300, Carlisle, Cumbria CA3 OQS U.K.

02 01 00 99 98 97 96  7 6 5 4 3 2 1

**British Library Cataloguing in Publication Data**

McFarlane, Graham, 1949–
    Christ and the Spirit : the doctrine of the incarnation
    according to Edward Irving
    1. Jesus Christ  2. Irving, Edward  3. Incarnation
    I. Title
    232.1

ISBN 0-85364-694-5

Typeset by Photoprint, Torquay, Devon.
Printed in Great Britain by BPC Wheatons Ltd, Exeter

# Contents

# Acknowledgements

Certain authors, speaking of their works, say, 'my book,' 'my commentary,' 'my history,' . . . They resemble middle class people who have a house of their own, and always have 'my house' on their tongue. They would do better to say, 'our book,' 'our commentary,' 'our history,' . . . because there is in them usually more of other people's than their own.

Pascall, *Pensées* #43.

This is not 'my book'. Its existence owes as much to others as it does to myself. It began its life as a PhD thesis submitted to King's College, the University of London, where were it not for those who believed in sharing home and self, the troughs and isolation of research would have been that much more difficult to bear. A special thanks to Ronnie and Caroline, Charles and Alison, Jean-Marc and Jenny, Kenny and Shona.

Neither can it be 'my book' for it grew out of discussion, argument, advice and criticism from a very intimate coterie which met weekly at the Research Institute in Systematic Theology at King's.

In addition, the theological content of this book cannot be claimed to be 'mine'. Research under the supervision and tutelage of Professor Colin Gunton was a pleasure I had the opportunity to enjoy. I am indebted to him for the way in which he invested his time and thoughts, as well as for introducing me to Edward Irving. This book is especially not 'mine' since it is only due to Colin's persistent encouragement that a thesis has been turned into a book.

I am greatly indebted to the Whitefield Institute for its financial support during my research years. Without it there would have been 'no' book.

Lastly, this book owes its beginning and end to three very special people: to my parents whose love and support throughout my theological training deserve more than thanks, and to my wife who has become my companion on this road less-travelled, and that has made all the difference.

# FOREWORD by Colin Gunton

It is a mark of the genius of Karl Barth that whilst reading in a history of theology a critical reference to Edward Irving's teaching that the Son of God assumed our sinful humanity, he decided that the nineteenth-century scot had something important to say. It is, correspondingly, a mark of Edward Irving's genius that he advocated at considerable cost, a doctrine that is essential to the Christian gospel and yet had been rejected or neglected for much of western theological history, both Catholic and Evangelical.

A number of attempts have recently been made to re-appropriate Irving's theology, notably in a wide-ranging study by Gordon Strachan. In this book by Graham McFarlane, however, we now have a full length investigation into the relation of pneumatology to christology by one who we must now acknowledge to be a ground-breaking theologian. The treatment of the third article is one of the marks of the standing or falling of a theology, to which pneumatology is the key.

In this book, the central topic of the person of Christ is approached by means of an examination of the two indispensable constituent loci, the doctrines of God and of man. As is being increasingly discovered, the way in which the doctrine of the Trinity is construed forms the essential background to a christology. For otherwise we could not give adequate account of the divine Saviour. Correlatively, unless we have a theological understanding of what it is to be human, the Lord's sharing of our condition becomes a mere abstraction.

In his study of Edward Irving's christology, Dr McFarlane explores essential historical and theological dimensions to

ix

Irving's treatment of these issues. His subject's relation to the western tradition is interestingly explored with some reference to the influence of Coleridge, and the part played by the will in Irving's understanding of the human condition. Similarly, the treatment of the person of Christ in relation not only to the Holy Spirit but also to Irving's understanding of the soul of Jesus as the crucial point, reveals both the depth and the idiosyncrasies of his subject.

Dr McFarlane opines that Irving is not one of the 'giants', but whatever we make of that judgement, he emphasises that we have someone whose major contribution should not be neglected. More importantly, he reminds us that we can be too dominated by accounts in the history of theology written, if not by, then in the light of those who have so far appeared to be the 'winners'. One of the most interesting aspects of this study is the awareness it shows of Irving's social and theological context. This is the world in which we are tempted to think of as the stage on which Schleiermacher dominates. He may have done so far but we must not forget that in every age of the church there have been faithful theologians who have resisted fashionable trends. May they not be in the end of much greater long-term significance?

King's College, London
March, 1996

# Introduction

Two roads diverged in a yellow wood,
And sorry I could not travel both
And be one traveler, long I stood
And looked down one as far as I could
To where it bent in the undergrowth;

Then took the other, as just as fair,
And having perhaps the better claim,
Because it was grassy and wanted wear;
Though as for that, the passing there
Had worn them really about the same,

And both that morning equally lay
In leaves no step had trodden black.
Oh, I kept the first for another day!
Yet knowing how way leads on to way,
I doubted if I should ever come back.

I shall be telling this with a sigh
Somewhere ages and ages hence
Two roads diverged in a wood, and I –
I took the one less traveled by,
And that has made all the difference.[1]

To change our standpoint is to transform our habits of thought. It is not to exchange one theory for another, but to change the basis of all theory. To achieve this must . . . be a long, co-operative process; a stumbling advance in country where there are no beaten paths to follow, and where every step may lead us astray.[2]

There seems to be something innately human about being distrustful of the unfamiliar yet at the same time of being

1

attracted to it. We are so wary of another's point of view, so quick to defend our own, so indisposed to the unfamiliar and untried, and yet all the time searching out for the newer and the better. On the whole, however, we are more likely to remain with the tried and tested than go with the new. Why is it that we are so unwilling to detach ourselves from the herd and try out uncharted paths? The answer may lie in the fact that our own ideas and 'habits of thought' are not so representative of lightly held opinions as they are of our very selves and the way in which we understand the world and make sense of it, and ultimately, ourselves. Our beliefs are part of the 'me' in relation to 'you', 'it' or 'them'. If this is so, then it is hardly surprising that the process by which we come to accept another's point of view is often a tortuous affair, fraught with difficulties: for in that process we are not exchanging new theories so much as questioning the very way in which we perceive ourselves. Such are the dynamics involved in the human need to understand and make sense of its own being and environment.

It is hardly surprising, then, that this same *modus operandi* is to be found throughout the history of Christian doctrine. There is no single expression of truth, no commonly held set of watertight beliefs. Rather, there is development and diversity. We should expect this when we consider that in the various Christian understandings of reality we find a common theme: at the very heart of Christian faith is a fundamentally personal assertion, namely, that truth comes to us in and through a person, Jesus Christ. With this notion comes a certain degree of obscurity, for, like a person, truth cannot be apportioned into neat definitions and, like a person it defies ultimate dogmatic categories. It can be as self-effacing as it can be revealing. Indeed, it is almost more helpful to describe truth in terms of what it is *not* than by means of a comprehensive series of assertions. Or additionally, the way of truth may be the way of silence, where more can be communicated in the silence that exists between friends than in the din of excessive chatter: the way of truth can be as contemplative as it is narratory.

Within the history of Christian thought there has been a

period of excessive chatter. Much of the dialogue has proven unable to deliver the illumination promised. Contemporary theologians straddle an exciting time of transition as old conversations give way to new ones. Neglected contributors in the theological narrative have begun to take on a new perspective. As the modern paradigm has begun to crumble, one viable option is to look to previous thinkers, by-passed in their own time but now being recognized as having something to say. There has been a renaissance of such theologians. It is almost as though they were fated to speak out of time: to be rejected by their own peers only to be recognized for their prophetic vision by subsequent generations.

One such figure is Edward Irving, and not him alone. Threads from his life are woven into the lives of John McLeod Campbell and Thomas Erskine of Linlathen. In various ways all three knew what it was to be rejected by the authorities of their day, and yet, all three are being increasingly read and recognized as having been incisive commentators on their own theological communities with something for us today.

What, then, of Irving? Why the interest in him? He is no theological giant, but neither is he an irrelevant figure: few theologians can be called a *cause célèbre* to the degree Irving knew. Yet it is not his infamy that is of interest here. Rather, running through the pages of this book is the belief that Irving detected a deadly peril facing traditional Christian teaching concerning both the doctrine of God as Trinity and the doctrine of the incarnation of the Son of God. Both doctrines were being increasingly deemed irrelevant and were being increasingly undermined. What marks Irving out for study is the response he gave to such criticisms. What makes him relevant today is the way in which he identified the end that would be reached were contemporary theologians to pursue their thinking. He was, by and large, correct in his conclusions. Yet what makes him even more interesting is the answer he sought to give. There is something clean in the way he cuts through all the issues in order to identify the two central elements of his faith: that we meet the threefoldness of God in the act of incarnation, and that the Son becomes incarnation by the power of the Spirit. For Irving, the two are intimately related.

The modern reader may be excused for blinking at such obvious theses, but it must be remembered that Western theologians have, by and large, never developed any significant relation between the doctrine of God the Trinity of Father, Son and Spirit and the doctrine of the incarnation. The two have tended to be treated separately, or at best, in a binitarian manner, with reference solely to the relation of Father and Son. It is a sad comment on Western theology to say that the person and role of the Spirit in relation to Jesus Christ and to the God of Jesus Christ, has never been satisfactorily demonstrated. This is surely significant given the fact that from our textual evidence there appears to be an intimate relation between the Spirit, Jesus Christ and the God of Jesus Christ.

Why has this relation not been expanded in any significant manner? The answer lies, perhaps, in the fact that we tend to develop our christology in an individualistic manner, in which we tend to think of Jesus Christ as an isolated and autonomous individual rather than as one in permanent relation to others. Consequently, Western christology tends to separate the doctrine of God as Father, Son and Spirit from its understanding of the incarnation. As a result, the place of the Spirit has become more and more obsolete until, in some major interpretations, the Spirit is completely redundant, despite the gospel witness.

The concern of this book, is with the place attributed to the Spirit in the incarnation, as given by Edward Irving. Irving is of interest because he holds together his doctrine of God the Trinity alongside his understanding of the incarnation in such a way as to make sense of the Spirit's place in the redemptive narratives. As Macmurray points out above, such a procedure demanded that Irving enter relatively uncharted territory 'where every step may lead us astray'. The task is set before us: to present a meaningful interpretation of the Spirit's role in the incarnation whilst holding onto the doctrine of God the Trinity. This is the goal Irving strove to establish, and like Macmurray, I have to admit that such a development in Western theology will be arrived at only after a 'long, co-operative process', a process which has begun to gain momentum in the latter part of the twentieth century.

It has been a great encourgement to discover that Edward Irving facilitates part of this process. He is no radical thinker in the sense that he proposes ideas that undermine traditionally accepted formulae. Quite the reverse: Irving may be understood as unfolding what has been in the tradition from its very genesis.

The structure of the book is such in order to highlight the way in which Irving understands the two fundamental components of his christology from within his tradition: the being of God and human being. For Irving both doctrines may be understood only through a prism or hermeneutic that is both christological and pneumatological: we understand God and ourselves to the degree we understand the Son and the Spirit.

It is hoped, then, that Irving's doctrine of Christ may be presented as a means by which our christological possibilities are expanded to realize the place we may give to the Spirit in the incarnation as well as to both Father and Son. As a result, Irving's insights may assist those who feel, nervously, that the traditional form of christology has met its 'judgement day'[3] and that 'we have seen the best of our time'.[4] It is my hope, rather, that this does not necessarily need to be 'judgement' day, but simply a new morning of theological possibilities.

## Notes

[1] R Frost, 'The Road Not Taken', *The Poetry of Robert Frost*, London: Jonathan Cape, 1976, 105.
[2] J Macmurray, *The Self as Agent*, London: Faber and Faber Limited, 1957, 85.
[3] E Dickenson, *Collected Poems*, New York: Routledge, 1982, 112.
[4] W Shakespeare, *King Lear*, Scene 1 Act 2.

# Part 1

# Irving's Doctrine of Divine Being

## Introduction

> What is it that we know so well and cannot speak? What is it
> that we want to say and cannot tell? What is it that keeps
> swelling in our hearts its grand and solemn music, that is aching
> in our throats, that is pulsing like a strange, wild grape, through
> all the conduits of our blood, that maddens us with its exultant
> and intolerable joy and that leaves us tongueless, wordless,
> maddened by our fury to the end? We do not know. All that we
> know is that we lack a tongue that could reveal, a language that
> could perfectly express the wild joy swelling to a music in our
> heart, the wild pain welling to a strong ache in our throat, the
> wild cry mounting to a madness in our brain, the thing, the
> word, the joy we know so well, and cannot speak?[1]

It is perhaps not by coincidence that at the heart of Christian
faith lies a drive to communicate, an urge to proclaim good
news. There is a sense of enthusiasm and excitement. We
want to articulate something important. Sometimes we get
the message across well and our language serves as a bridge
between speaking and understanding. The more simple the
message the easier it is to understand. However, when we
broach the unfamiliar and unarticulated, we begin to touch
on the boundaries of language: our words do not always
match up to the feelings, thoughts and aspirations within us.

Perhaps this is where the novelist and the theologian
meet. Both seek to express the deeper issues of life.
Consequently, both tend to feel keenly the limitations of
language. There is almost something mysterious about the
way language works: it is both revealing and effacing.
Indeed, we take our language skills so much for granted that

9

we miss the miracle of communication.[2] Without language
we would, literally and verbally, not *be*. However, at the
same time, language needs us! As Don Cupitt reminds us,
language requires both temporality, a sense of history in
order to understand, and materiality, 'some sort of body or
material vehicle'.[3] We, it would appear, depend on each
other!

The mystery, then, lies in its self-effacing character: it has
its being in its revealing. The miracle of language is
expressed both in the creative act and in the fecundity and
subsequent creativity to which language lends itself. A word
becomes a key which unlocks a world of ideas; ideas, in turn,
take root, develop and shape further horizons of thought. If
this human skill manifests itself in the capacity to express
and identify, then its supreme expression lies in the ability to
articulate that which never before has been said. So ventured one of the earliest Christian theologians:

> In the beginning was the Word, and the Word was with God,
> and the Word was God. He was in the beginning with God . . .
> In him was life, and the life was the light of men . . . And the
> Word became flesh and dwelt among us, full of grace and truth
> . . . The law was given through Moses; grace and truth came
> through Jesus Christ.[4]

Never before had such an event required expression. Something hitherto unspoken broke through the established
markers concerning God's being. What now did it mean to
talk of a God whose Word is expressed in the very stuff and
matter of human being? Surely not that Jesus Christ introduces us for the first time to an understanding of God? After
all, God predates the man Jesus from Nazareth. Rather,
'Jesus becomes a route to rethink the doctrine of God . . .
Jesus Christ "intersects" with those understandings of and
questions about God which human beings already have,
calling into question what is known and compelling a
rethinking of received conceptions.'[5]

Obviously, this initial encounter demands some kind
of response from those who have met with God in Jesus
Christ. We generally identify this response to be the task of

theology. This task demands a re-focussing of our language simply because we are forced to talk about God.

Such a development has never been simple. Historically, this inquiry into the character and nature of God has had two major concerns, aptly summed up by Colin Gunton as the desire to maintain the distinction between the One, the Three and the Many.[6] Firstly, it was concerned to maintain that God is one. In Jesus we do not meet two or three gods. However, this was circumscribed by the equally strong desire to articulate God's diversity as Father, Son and Spirit. Despite the human proclivity to stress either the unity or threeness, each at the expense of the other, it is the doctrine of God as Trinity that has become the interpretative tool by which we make sense of both Jesus and God. As a result, the doctrine of the Trinity has traditionally been held as a necessary element of Christian belief. In some way, the history of the man Jesus from Nazareth is caught up in the very identity of God, an identity we have come to realize in a trinitarian manner.

Perhaps it is helpful to express this relationship in terms similar to that between object and language. The object in question, the life and death or faith and teaching of Jesus, finds best expression and meaning through the language of the Trinity. Whilst faith is placed in Jesus Christ, we understand what he has done for us in light of the doctrine of the Trinity.[7] Whatever it was and however we may put it, in the very earliest experiences of God in Jesus Christ onwards there was something that demanded a distinction to be made about God, as Father, Son and Spirit, in order to make sense of the kind of saving action and good news that was encountered in Jesus. This trinitarian interpretation helped the followers of Jesus to make sense of God. Thus, on the basis of their experience in and through Jesus Christ, the early Christian communities confessed faith in a God who is both one and three.

## Unity and Diversity

It is this same intimate link between what we believe about Jesus Christ and the subsequent theological expression of

God as Trinity that concerns us as we turn to consider the foundations of Edward Irving's doctrine of Christ. What is so significant about Irving is the fact that he wrote at a time when most people believed that the proper procedure was to separate the doctrine of the Trinity from what could be said about Christ. By the time of Schleiermacher, such a distinction was taken as a given. Irving, then, stands out sharply as one who opposed such procedure. Rather, he sought to unite the two in a perhaps more radical manner than has hitherto been presented within his own Western, theological tradition.

The manner by which Irving achieves this reflects both his continuity with, as well as his difference from, his own theological tradition. The former is reflected in the priority he gives to the biblical story of Jesus Christ, both as the incarnate Word of John and as the inspired man of the Synoptics. The one we come to know as Father, Son and Spirit is the God of Scripture. The practical task of identifying God's being distinguishes the Christian God from all others: he is not the God of the philosophers. First and foremost he is the God of Scripture.

However, the way in which we interpret things is always moulded by the context in which we find ourselves. For Irving, this context demanded a hands-on solution: knowledge of God must be practical; it must arouse the believer to service and devotion for God. In this Irving follows his Calvinistic tradition. Like Calvin's, his doctrine of God is not lofty doctrine. He has little to say on the nature of God in any abstract sense, and does not give any systematic account of the existence, nature and attributes of God.

Who, then, is God? As noted earlier, he is the one we meet in Scripture—and who encounters us in our own histories. Whilst complete knowledge of God is beyond human ken, knowledge of the *mysterium trinitatis* is given through the act of incarnation, as well as in the ongoing action of God in redemption, starting with the church and going out to the wider created order. Thus, Irving talks about God in a way very similar to that of earlier theologians such as Basil who affirmed that 'the divine nature is too exalted to be perceived as objects of enquiry are to be perceived,' and thus we are 'guided in the investigation of the divine nature by its operations.'[8]

Like Calvin, Irving understands the doctrine of the Trinity to be a postulate of the believer's profoundest religious experience, given in the very act of salvation.[9] Yet unlike the theological methods adopted by his contemporaries, Schleiermacher and Coleridge, Irving makes the doctrine of the Trinity the very foundation for his entire understanding of Christ and therefore for any meaningful and adequate doctrine of salvation.[10] Thus he argues:

> If the doctrine of the Trinity be the foundation of all orthodox doctrine . . . If the Trinity be the only eternally existing substance, from the operation of whom all things that are have been created out of nothing that is seen, but out of the invisible will, word, and Spirit of the Godhead; if all things that are, and everything that is, be but the shewing forth of the Divine Essence of the Triune God . . . then do I say, that every act of the preacher of the gospel is incomplete, yea, is not an act of preaching Christ, which doth not contain the three offices of the Divine Persons, and display them.[11]

We can identify two important issues here. Firstly, Irving moves away from Augustine's emphasis on divine unity which tends to flatten any distinction between the Father, Son and Spirit.[12] God's history has become our history in such a way that we *have* to create space in which to talk about God as Father, Son and Spirit in very distinct ways. Secondly, whilst Irving argues strongly that the church's experience of God reveals something of the divine mystery he does so not from any a priori philosophical belief about God, but rather from his understanding of scripture. Such an approach reflects both continuity with his theological inheritance, as well as the means by which he safeguards his doctrine of God from any abstract speculation.

In what way, though, does Irving differ from his tradition? In order to answer this it is necessary to take a closer look at Irving's doctrine of God and how he establishes a role for the Spirit in his understanding of incarnation. Here we touch on the very core of our present concern: showing how Irving develops his understanding of the Spirit, both in relation to the being of God and in the act of incarnation.

## The Grace of God

Irving's thoughts on the doctrine of God as Trinity were given shape and form in 1825 in a series of sermons on the Trinity, preached to his congregation in Hatton Garden, London. Little attention was given to them then or in 1828 when they were first put into print. Subsequent biographers and scholars have failed to pick up the creative expression Irving gives to his understanding of God. Subsequently, the importance of these germinal sermons to Irving's theology has gone relatively unnoticed. The only exception to this trend was with Irving's early biographer. She writes, when commenting upon these early sermons on the Trinity:

> These sermons, though of a very different character from those bursts of bold and splendid oratory by which the preacher had made his great reputation, are perhaps more remarkable than any of his other productions.[13]

However, this overall inattention is wholly in character with the events surrounding Irving's life. The heated examination within which his doctrine of the human nature of Christ was developed was itself divorced from the wider doctrine of God being expounded in these early sermons. It is, however, uncertain whether a full appreciation of Irving's doctrine of God would have aided or abetted the final outcome, for it reflected the same degree of individuality as found in his later christological sermons.[14]

Such streaks of individuality are manifested in the fact that whilst it is for the many to accede, only the few inquire. What is acceptable for the former often remains unsatisfactory for the latter. Thus for Irving his theology marks him out as one of the few. Whilst the many were content to give assent to their credal belief in one God who is Father, Son and Spirit, Irving's interest lay with both the ontological, that is, concerned primarily with being, as well as with the ontical, that is concerned with entities and facts about them.[15] With particular respect to this doctrine of God he sought not so much to explain the existence of God as one and many, as to give theological expression to the creative activity of Father, Son and Spirit in incarnation and redemption. Therefore, his is not an explicit analysis of God's being. Rather, it is a theological concern aimed at a specifically soteriological end. It is concerned with the dynamics of salvation, the manner by which the grace of God comes with assurance to us humans in our separation from him.

However, Irving is also concerned to outline the subject of grace. For if human beings are the objects of divine grace, from when and from whom does this grace flow? Within what context, then, may we identify this grace and by what means may we be certain that we are indeed the beneficiaries of divine grace? He has a very practical end in mind.

Irving's answer incorporates two distinct criteria. Firstly, that the quality of grace is contingent upon its source: it is God's grace. Thus, Irving is at pains to establish the Son's divinity at all costs in order to contest the Arian, Socinian and Unitarian notions that the Son is not God but only an exalted creature. Secondly, that we may identify the source of grace solely from the act of incarnation: it is God's saving action in Christ that delineates the perimeters for our understanding of God.

Both criteria are united in a series of sermons based upon Ephesians 12, 'Grace to you and peace from our Father and Lord Jesus Christ.' In these sermons, he focuses on the relation between the Father and Son, with specific stress upon the identity and status of the Son. It would appear, then, that both chronologically and theologically, Irving establishes what he believes about the Son before he goes on to expand his belief about the Spirit.

Irving approaches the divine mystery in a twofold manner. When arguing for divine unity and equality of Father, Son and Spirit, he seeks to establish the divinity of the Son. The divinity of the Spirit stands or falls with that of the Son. In addition, the theological rule, *opera trinitatis ad extra indivisa sunt*, that is, the external operations of the Trinity are indivisible, enables Irving to clarify his basic belief. When establishing the plurality and individuality of the divine persons, he apportions to each a specific activity within the overall plan of salvation. The unity of divine action *ad extra* highlights the distinction of divine being *ad intra*. The unity and diversity of God is reflected in the manner by which he saves us. But it also reveals the diversity of operation. Thus, our knowledge of God corresponds to the way in which he makes himself known in and through Jesus Christ.

In his sermons on Ephesians, Irving focuses specifically upon the relationship between the Father and the Son. However, we should not think that he is uninterested in the Spirit. Theologically, he believes that the Spirit is 'self-effacing'. The Spirit defies direct examination.[16] This is not an excuse for irrationality concerning the Spirit. Irving is not satisfied to leave things at this. He is as interested in the dynamic by which his credo holds together as in its dogmatic content. Thus, he seeks to give as full an expression as possible to the way in which God relates to us. This will include the Spirit. It is because he seeks to combine this with a full-blooded understanding of salvation that the identity of Christ takes precedence, but in a way not divorced from the Spirit. The means he uses involves highlighting the character and action of the self-effacing Spirit of God. Irving is not blind at all to the tensions involved in such a method:

> And as it is a sign of infirmity and sickness to be talking about our health, and economising our powers of action, so it is a sign of weakness in the spirit to be talking about the Spirit and searching into His office, and feeling for his influence.[17]

Whether or not Irving is correct in this conclusion is of no great concern here. What is of importance is the foundation he lays for future theological development. It is this foundational component of the Spirit that subsequent commentators on Irving have ignored, namely, the self-effacing role of the Spirit in any act of God. As a result, the significance of Irving's appreciation for the being and action of God the Spirit in creation, incarnation and redemption has been overlooked. However, before we can explore this further we must, first, turn our attention to the means by which Irving establishes the identity and divinity of the Son. Such a task introduces us to the hermeneutical problem implicit in the church's christological debate: whether or not 'the divine that has appeared on earth and reunited man with God' is 'identical with the supreme divine, which rules heaven and earth, or is . . . a demigod?'[18]

When we turn to his Trinity sermons, we find Irving applying himself to this question by means of the Son's relation to the Father. He focuses particularly upon Ephesians 1:2 where he talks about God, alongside the grace that is given in his saving action towards us. Moreover, the source of this grace, despite the plurality of persons, is unequivocally singular, pointing towards the notion of oneness. If the grace itself is neither shared nor divided between the Father and Son, how does it come into being?

> Seeing that it is not in the way of share or division that the grace and peace cometh from these two Divine fountains, it must be in the way of passage or transition from the one to the other . . . from God our Father to our Lord Jesus Christ.[19]

For Irving, God the Father is the supreme subject of all divine action and whilst God the Father is the sufficient cause of himself, he is neither individual nor independent. God is Father because God is also Son. Thus, the source of grace is neither divided nor independent. Both the Father and the Son define the source of this grace. Irving expresses the relation between Father and Son in a hierarchical or monarchical manner. It becomes the key that unlocks the problem of God's being as Trinity in a way that is both dynamic and interpersonal. The Father is both prior to and equal with the Son. As Irving puts it:

> I lay it down as the first principle in all sound theology that the fullness of the Father is poured into the Son, and returneth back through the Holy Spirit unto the Father, all creatures being by the Holy Spirit brought forth of the Son, in order to express a part of the Father's will and of His delight in His Son, which they do by union with the Son, promised through the Holy Spirit.[20]

It is this principle of causality which Irving uses to maintain the distinction he understands to exist between the Father and the Son. His understanding of incarnation, where the Son's obedience to the Father is revealed, enables Irving to interpret the Father as the means by which we gain insight into the mystery of divine being. Like Athanasius,[21] Irving affirms the divine identity and status of the Son from the title of God as Father. This major thrust of his argument is very similar to the patristic defence against Arius. Yet Irving unpacks the traditional argument with the secondary relationship between the Son and Word. Each shall be examined separately for the sake of simplicity and clarity. Our attention here, however, is on the place attributed to each in the analysis of God's being. This is not an attempt to explain away the *mysterium trinitatis*, for whilst the Trinity may be above reason, ultimately, it is not against it. Rather, his method reflects the overall goal of Irving's thinking: to discern the means by which God's grace is given to fallen human beings. Consequently, before he presents the means by which this grace is made available, he sets his mind to establish, deductively, the quality of being that exists between the Father and the Son.

## The Son and the Word

The function of language, for Irving, does not lie in making a word work 'terribly hard' and rewarding it for doing so, but rather in the ease and precision by which a word expresses and illumines, thus giving understanding. Like Alice, Irving questions any extravagant claims attributed to particular words:

> 'When *I* use a word,' Humpty Dumpty said in a rather scornful tone, 'it means just what I choose it to mean—neither more nor less.'
>
> 'The question is' said Alice, 'whether you *can* make words mean different things.'
>
> The question is,' said Humpty Dumpty, 'which is to be master—that's all . . .'

'That's a great deal to make one word mean,' Alice said in a thoughtful tone.

'When I make a word do a lot of work like that,' said Humpty Dumpty, 'I always pay it extra.'

'Oh!' said Alice. She was too much puzzled to make any other remark.

'Ah, you should see 'em come round me of a Saturday night,' Humpty Dumpty went on, wagging his head gravely from side to side, 'for to get their wages, you know.'[22]

There is an intimate relation between language and thought, word and object. We see this most clearly in the way Irving understands the function of 'God-talk'. It must be earthed and grounded in the Christ-event, or, to be more precise, in the incarnation of the Son of God. Throughout his Trinity sermons the dynamic of incarnation underlies Irving's entire argument, moulding the concepts that finally express his doctrine of God as Trinity.

What, for instance, is the significance of talking about God as 'the Word' when talking about the second person of the Trinity? Since Irving derives the basis of knowledge about God from God's own gracious activity towards us in incarnation, he is adamant in his answer:

> There could be no manifestation of the grace of God in the purpose of redemption from the simple knowledge of Christ as the Word.[23]

To describe Jesus Christ solely as God the Word, is inadequate in expressing fully the nature of the one we come to know through the Christ. It fails to communicate the full impact of what God really does in Christ, and therefore impoverishes our doctrine of salvation, intrinsic to any knowledge of God since we come to know him only as sinners rescued by grace. Irving identifies two significant implications in holding to a christology that is merely Word-centred. Firstly, God's being as Word affords only the idea of will, and as such, bears no revelation of grace, which is the attribute of a person, not a mere will. Whilst Irving places great stress on the notion of will, he does make a distinction between person and will. For him, the identity of Christ as Word can only express, at best, his ability to participate in and reveal the Father's will, similar to the way in which human words express the thoughts of their subject. However, in the same way that our own words are not essentially part of us, so God's Word is not necessarily essentially related to nor capable of expressing God fully.

This is an important distinction which leads us to the second issue. How is Irving able to show that the Son expresses something about God which the Word cannot express? The issue centres around the notion of love—the full and free love of one person to another. If we identify Christ solely as Word, then this description fails to express the identity of the second *person* of the Trinity, and, more importantly, who God is both in his being-for-others and as himself. If the Word suggests one who shares in and expresses the Father's will, then it is only through the notion of Son that we confront the notion of love. Irving puts it this way:

> The Word doth express His participation of all the Father's counsels, and His office in revealing them all: but the Son is that which expresseth His full possession of the Father's undivided affections, wrapping up in Himself all that love upon which the universe was to lean, as He wrapped up in his name of the Word all that wisdom by which the universe was to subsist. If it be an essential part of the eternal purpose of the Godhead revealed by Christ, that it contains the fullness of the Father's love in surrendering, as well as of the Father's wisdom in manifesting Christ, then I say that He who was surrendered must have been in the full possession of all the Father's love, as well as a sharer of all the Father's wisdom; or that He must have been Son as well as Word from all eternity. There is the same connexion between His office of Prophet in time and His personality of Word from eternity, as there is between His office of Saviour in time and of Son from eternity,—the one expressing a portion of the incommunicable wisdom of God which He was fraught withal; the other expressing a portion of the incommunicable love of God, whereof the fullness was poured into His single bosom, which can alone contain the ocean of its fullness.[24]

Of importance here is the priority given to the idea of relationships and the different relations involved with the two descriptions. God's being, as it were, extends beyond the simple need to communicate with someone outside himself in the way human beings do. Rather, God's being consists of internalized relations. Therefore, not only does God's being as Word convey a somewhat impersonal relation, but it is also unable to support the belief that at the very heart of the Christian message, personal redemption is to be found. It is only as Son that Christ receives the Father's love, and is therefore able to make this love, rather than a bare will, known to us.[25] The good news consists of a message of love, first and foremost.

### The Son and the Father

Irving has now established the first stage of his ontology: in order for the work of Christ to reveal anything more than bare will, God's being-for-us, if we can put it this way, must include both the creative capacity to communicate, as Word, and the capacity to love, as Son. Irving is now able to turn his attention to show how in the inner relationship between the Son and the Father we meet with divine equality. In so doing, he seeks to highlight the intimate relationship the one has with the other.

### The Son as Creature

The doctrine of the Trinity implies specific hermeneutical questions. If God is made known to us through the Son, the question to ask is whether this Son is identical with the God the Father or whether he is merely some kind of demi-god. One historical and repeated response has been given in the Arian, Socinian and Unitarian notion that the Son is not divine, but is a creature.

The problem of God's creatureliness, and it *is* a problem for those who confess an incarnated God, is addressed by Irving in relation to the doctrine of salvation. If the Son is a creature, even the highest of all creatures, even the one through whom all others come into being, then there are three consequences. Firstly, any act of divine affection upon one particular creature which does not extend to all other creatures will not elicit love and adoration, but rather excite:

> envy and disgust in all other creatures to behold God lavishing such excess fondness, and bestowing such amplitude of love upon one creature, and exalting him by such immeasurable titles and unparalleled honours unto His own immediate presence and fellowship and blessedness . . . This Socinianism is the destruction and death of all confidence of the creature towards God, and must of necessity beget distance and reserve when they behold such ravishment and blandishment upon one above the rest.[26]

Secondly, even a created Word is incapable of reflecting the perfect and complete image of the invisible God. Whereas the Word may reveal the will from which it proceeds, as a creature it is incapable of a complete revelation of God's will or mind. It affords only a visible creation, and a creaturely manifestation and understanding of that will. Fundamental to Irving's christology is the belief that nothing specifically created can fully reveal the Creator's character. The upshot of this, therefore, is that in ascribing more creaturely existence to Christ, whether as Word or as Son, God's trinitarian mystery remains hidden. Thus Irving argues:

> How can there be complete trust or assured love towards one whom we have no complete revelation of, I cannot conceive. I do not mean that it is necessary to comprehend God, in order to love Him and trust Him. You know how often I have exposed the profanity of such a thought as that we can comprehend God, or that He should be comprehensible . . . But if He is a creature that hath been manifested, then it is at best a work of God we have been contemplating, not God himself, who is still as much behind the veil as ever; and revelation is no revelation; and, in truth, there is not revelation made of God himself, but only of a creature of God.[27]

Thirdly, to claim that such a creature is commissioned by God for the purpose of revelation is of little consequence, for at best all that can be revealed is the creature's understanding of God, an understanding that is finite, no matter how capacious the creature's abilities. Therefore, no matter how exalted a creature, the Son remains a *creature*. Consequently, Irving perceptively argues that,

> (If) I am a piece of God's workmanship as well as he, (I) may teach him a lesson, as properly as he may teach me one. And the lesson I learn from him can in no wise obliterate the lesson I learn from myself. And if these disagree, then . . . I will cleave to my one intimate acquaintance with my dear self rather than to any message brought to me from afar by another, who is but a creature like myself.[28]

The significance of this point is not to be understated. It represents a defiant contemporary theological stand on Irving's part. Whilst prevailing theological methods were moving towards an anthropocentric hermeneutic, Irving radicalized the theocentric in an attempt to hold together what his contemporaries were pulling apart, namely, the doctrines of Christ and the Trinity. The post-modernity of Irving's thought is revealed in his stress on the manner of revelation, for it anticipates the more post-modern interpretation of the Trinity of Barth by nearly a century.[29] Although we have not reached a full explication of Irving's argument, we are already being introduced to the notion of the one who is both Revealed and Revealer. We now turn our attention to the manner by which he establishes the full divine status of the Son.

## The Son as Divine

Irving moves his argument towards its final goal. God's being as Word makes us privy solely to the bare will of God. It is only as a Son that Christ can communicate the full character of God the Father. However, his argument at this point remains open to Arian, Socinian and Unitarian interpretations; that strange tautology which envisages the Son to be a divine creature. It is now necessary to delineate how Irving affirms the ontological equality of the Son with the

Father, that is, how he understands the Son to be fully God. This he does by means of a twofold rejection.

Firstly, he rejects the notion that, 'Christ is a Divine person, the same in substance and equal in power and glory with the Father, but that he is not the Son from all eternity, but only from the day of his earthly generation, or from some higher date which is still in time.'[30] He returns once again to his central premise: we do not gain the full description of God's being from such a concept. In essence, it carries no ontological weight. The relations of fatherhood and sonship remain accidental and circumstantial. If the Son is dependent upon an origin in time for the purposes of both redemption and revelation, where do we find any essential and unchangeable knowledge of God?

> For when you say that Christ is not Son from eternity, you say that God is not a Father from eternity; and when you say that Christ is Son only with relation to the work of redemption, you say that God is Father only with relation to the same.[31]

Throughout his argument, Irving pushes his hermeneutic further in order to establish his description of the Trinity, one which relates to the true nature of God as Father, Son and Spirit. All the time it is one that also coheres with the Christian gospel. For as he argues, 'If God be not known as Father, save to fallen men, nor Christ as Son, as what are they known?' Certainly not as Will or Word, he continues, for although both are expressions of God, they reveal 'no love or parental care, goodness, no grace, expressed by that mode of stating and apprehending the relation between the everlasting Persons.'[32]

Fundamental to Irving's christology, therefore, is the belief that Jesus Christ is God's being as Son for us in such a way that we really do meet with the Father God through him. The Son is not an exalted agent: he is God, and for this to be the case, he must be fully God.

However, Irving is not content to rest at this. His concern also involves the grounds of sonship. How is he Son? In what manner does his sonship consist? Having addressed the origin of the Son's existence within time, and having found it insufficient to establish the idea of paternal love, Irving turns his attention to the idea he thinks most undermines the truth of the matter, namely that God's being as Son is derived 'from the eternal purpose of God, in which He gave Himself as an offering for sin—in that it is not essential to Him as the eternal Word, but belongs to Him as party in the everlasting covenant and all inclusive purpose of God.'[33] Now, to the casual reader this may appear to be theological hair-splitting! How can we talk of an eternal being who has a point of origin? Irving is astute enough to realize that the matter can still be twisted. Therefore, having thwarted the idea that the Son's origin is derived from a point in time, there still remains the need to clarify the exact manner of his eternal origination.

It may be good to remind ourselves at this point exactly what Irving's goal is: it is to establish the full divinity of the Son with the Father, in a manner consistent with the nature of salvation offered in the Christian gospel. Thus he is wrestling here with a rather subtle intrusion, as he nears the end of his critical analysis of those notions he considers to be less than adequate to establish his goal. He confronts here the notion that the identity of Christ as Son of God is derived from his being as Word rather than from his relation to the Father. If the Word is given superiority over the Son, then the office of the Son becomes a cognate of the divine will, and to teach that is to say that the ultimate ground of being is will rather than person. In addition, if we identify the Son in this way we really make null and void any real and essential union between the Father and the Son, because the Son does not originate from the being of the Father, but from the eternal covenant of God with his creation. As such, the Son is not eternal with the Father. Rather, he is an exalted creature.

Irving enjoys the manner by which he refutes the arguments of his opponents. Only if the Son is eternal and essential God can he both fulfil the divine purpose of redemption and reveal to us the relation of love between himself and the Father. And here we confront the significance of unlocking the mystery of divine being by means of the notion of grace. Perhaps Irving is at his best in the way

he connects the act of redeeming love with the subject of this
love, when he states that, 'the greatness of the grace is
according to the greatness of the love which was set aside'.[34]
There is something profound about such a simple insight. If
we are to know God's great love then the One in whom and
by whom it is known must be God. Thus the Son must be
identical in status with the Father. As Irving puts it:

> His pre-existence as the Son of God is essential; his pre-
> existence as the Word is not sufficient to constitute the purpose
> as I find it written in all the Scriptures. For this purpose is not a
> purpose of will only, but it is a purpose of goodness, and of
> grace, and of mercy, and of bounty,—in one word, it is a
> purpose of love, according to the good pleasure of His will . . .
> Now the relation of Word . . . gives us no idea of love, but of
> will only; and without the revelation of Father and Son, we have
> not that idea. Wherefore it is absolutely necessary to the
> formation of a purpose which should contain the infinitude of all
> grace, that the Father should have known Christ as Son in the
> act of His origination, and loved Him with the fullness of the
> love of God, in order that, when He was surrendered in the
> purpose, we might be able to discern the fullness of the grace of
> God unto all creation.[35]

Finally, we arrive at the goal. Christ's identity as Word is
insufficient to support a consistent doctrine of salvation. For
God to be known as a loving Father, the Christ must be his
eternal Son, and not merely his Word: the former has
priority over the latter. Only an eternal and essential
relationship between Father and Son establishes the true
character of the grace made available in Christian salvation.
It is the grace of *love*. Or, put more recently, 'The Son is the
*verbum cordis*, the meaning of the heart, the meaning of
intimacy and love'.[36]

Having defended his understanding of God's being as
Father and Son, Irving is now at liberty to move beyond the
reactive towards the proactive, and to construct his own
theological solution to the particular issues that have been
raised. However, in order to highlight the significance of
Irving's own solution, it may be helpful to turn to an earlier

response developed by the fourth century Greek theologians, Basil of Caeserea, Gregory of Nyssa and Gregory of Nazianzus. Between them they developed what has come to be regarded as the Church's orthodox, correct interpretation of divine being, and one which opened up a fuller appreciation of God's being as Spirit.

## A Point of Comparison

Since its origins the Christian faith has struggled to express adequately the very nature and character of God's being. Whilst editing and compiling the early oral traditions maintained by the first Christian communities, the gospel writers felt no strain in presenting Jesus, the Christ, in terms of equality with the God he made known as Father. Nor did they shrink from implying equal status to the one they knew and experienced as Spirit: one who was distinct both from the Father and Jesus Christ. With almost casual ease, they held in tension both the belief that in Jesus the man we meet the divine Son, and the confession of one God who is known through Christ, as Father, Son and Spirit.

This casual synthesis of the one and the many continues in the epistles, with references in doxology, benediction, opening and closing pleasantries, to an implied equality of persons. Yet, at no time do these writers express any hint of presumption in declaring their faith in a monotheistic God of Persons.[37] The sense of both one and many was, it seems, the logical conclusion from the church's experience of God. There was something about the Christian experience of God that embraced this seeming paradox. The early Christian communities' experience of God as Father, Son and Spirit long preceded any interpretation and explanation of God.

Such theological scrutiny was to become a major element in church thinking by the end of the apostolic era.[38] The need to develop language and ideas was a necessary aspect of church teaching if the faithful were to be enabled to affirm the unity and diversity of God's being. Thus, whilst it was a universal activity, it is in the Greek East that we find the most refined form of the doctrine of God which may, in turn, help establish the rightness, or orthodoxy, of Irving.

## The Cappadocian Fathers

In order to understand better Irving's contribution and development to the doctrine of God as Trinity, we turn, then, to the Cappadocians. This in itself is an important point of method, for it is all too easy to caricature differing theological opinions and pit one against the other. Due to the different traditions of new contexts wherein questions and solutions are reviewed, reconsidered and reconstructed, the theologian must develop in harmony with, rather than by opposition to what is inherited from the past. This is most certainly the case when we consider the different theological concepts which have moulded trinitarian doctrine. Perhaps the frustrating factor in this is that we do not discover homogenized unity but mysterious diversity. Kenneth Surin puts it well when he points out that there is an 'unbridgeable dichotomy between Eastern and Western trinitarianism,' and goes on to add that, 'It must be acknowledged that tradition has given us *two* possible approaches to the mystery of the Trinity, both of which are perfectly orthodox, but which reflect undeniably different attitudes to the mystery.'[39]

If that which creates and moulds history can be ultimately attributed to the *divine afflatus*—for who can teach great genius, what theory produces leaders?—then the emergence of the Cappadocian Fathers is to be understood as one historic moment which was to mould future theological development. They were the inheritors of the church's one truly ecumenical statement of faith, the Council of Nicea's Creed (325 AD), and continued its empirical and deductive method.[40] They argued from the Christian experience of God as Father and Son to formulate their doctrine of God which was to be vindicated at the Council of Constantinople (381 AD). On the one hand they affirmed the distinction between the divine and the human, and on the other they affirmed the belief that the church's experience of God reveals something of the divine mystery.

The task fell to the Cappadocians to steer the church between the Scylla of Jewish monotheism and its Christian counterpart, Sabellianism, and the Charybdis of Greek polytheism and its Christian counterpart, Arianism. Their task was to avoid these two opposing theologies whilst also to express their own understanding of God as Trinity. In so doing, they were to arrive finally at a theology which was to prove 'a bulwark both against Arian subordinationism and against Sabellian unipersonalism,'[41] that is, that the Son is a creature and that God is only one but can wear three different masks, as it were, respectively.

The task fell first to Basil of Caeserea to establish an adequate framework within which to talk meaningfully about God as both one and three without implying either of the above dangers. This involved developing an understanding of being which, to do so, required a development in language which could actually facilitate talk of the one God who is also three.

In order to avoid Sabellianism in which the three persons are merely three roles or masks of the one God, Basil sought to speak of Father, Son and Spirit as three actual beings, rather than mere roles. However, at this time, 'person' did not carry this meaning. In fact, it had the unfortunate meaning of 'role' or 'mask', rather akin to actor. As such, it was not a permanent identity, and therefore hardly suitable for the purposes Basil was seeking. What Basil did do was to perform a major re-interpretation in understanding, no mean feat, in order to establish a view of reality and being which gave full meaning to the word 'person'. This he did by developing the world-view, or metaphysic, he inherited from his great theological predecessor, Athanasius, who argued that a thing's concrete individuality (its *hypostasis*) means simply that it is (its *ousia*). What Basil did, then, was to identify what was previously understood as a mask or role, namely 'person', with the new meaning derived from *hypostasis*, that is, the concreteness of a thing.

Now, this may appear somewhat complicated. Perhaps it is. But what Basil did was to bring together two distinct meanings in order to create a hybrid concept. He gave to the impersonal *hypostasis* a personal meaning derived from 'person', thus upgrading it. At the same time he gave to 'person' the stability derived from the concept of *hypostasis*, thus stabilizing it and giving it an ontological status by virtue of the relationship *hypostasis* has with *ousia*.

Secondly, not only were words upgraded, but the identity of the Son was also upgraded. At least, a degrading notion derived from Origen was excluded, namely the notion that the Son was an intermediate being, the kind of mediator who was less than the Father. Rather, the Son was to be attributed an equal status with the Father.[42]

Christian theology was at last equipped with a language which enabled it to talk of God as both one and three. The unity of God was now to be found in the oneness and the diversity was to be found in the relations. There were not three different gods, but rather the one God who is to be distinguished by his three particular relations of Father, Son and Spirit. In technical language, that which unites God is the common being or *ousia* and that which distinguishes the three is the particular, the individual relations or *hypostases*.[43] Thus Basil states:

> The term *ousia* is common, like goodness or Godhead, or any similar attribute; while *hypostasis* is contemplated in the special property of Fatherhood, Sonship, or the power to sanctify.[44]

With this, the teaching of Sabellius was finally refuted: God is not three masks, but one who is at one and the same time, always, Father, Son and Spirit. They are united in their commonly shared being and their subsequent undivided activity.

This divine activity operates in a particular way. In his *Theological Orations*, Gregory of Nazianzus argues for a very specific form of operation we know as monarchianism, that is, like a monarch and the subordinate roles under him. Gregory is clear that there is such a monarchy between the relations of the Father, Son and Spirit. What, then, is it?

Firstly, he dismisses the idea of an anarchia or polyarchia. Rather, there is a form of relations between the divine persons that reveals a sort of hierarchy. Thus, Gregory writes,

Monarchy is that which we hold in honour. It is, however, a
Monarchy that is not limited to one Person . . . Unity having
from all eternity arrived by motion at Duality, found rests in
Trinity. This is what we mean by Father and Son and Holy
Ghost. The Father is the Begetter and the Emitter: without
passion . . . and without reference to time, and not in a corporal
manner. The Son is the Begotten, and the Holy Ghost the
Emission . . . Let us confine ourselves within our limits, and
speak of the Unbegotten and the Begotten and that which
proceeds from the Father.[45]

Put simply, the thing that marks the one from the other is
the relation or the 'coming to be' each has to the other.[46]
This is described in terms of monarchy, in that the Father is
understood to be the cause of the Son and the Spirit: the Son
is begotten, the Spirit proceeds, each from the Father. Due
to the fact that these descriptions belong to the relations or
persons, and not to the very essence or being of God, the
Cappadocians were able to ascribe this idea of a monarchy
or causality to the Trinity without implying any subordination in the very being or essence of God. In this way, they
could accord the idea of 'being begotten' to the Son without
implying that he must have had a beginning, and hence that
he was a creature of some sort or other.

To the modern reader this notion of causality, and the hint
to some kind of subordination within the Godhead, may
appear somewhat alarming. We have, after all, become
accustomed to the idea that all persons are totally equal.
What has to be remembered here is that all three are equally
God by virtue of being the same being. Therefore, although
they exist differently—as Father, Son and Spirit—all three
are equally God. This idea of causality was derived, however, not from theological abstraction but from the Christian
experience of God. God was experienced as Father, Son and
Spirit in a single cooperating activity which came to be
understood as derived from the unity of will between all
three.

We do not learn that the Father does something on his own, in
which the Son does not co-operate. Or again, that the Son acts
on his own without the Spirit. Rather does every operation

which extends from God to creation and is designated according to our differing conceptions of it have its origin in the Father, proceed through the Son, and reach its completion in the Holy Spirit. It is for this reason that the word for the operation is not divided among the persons involved. For the action of each in any matter is not separate and individualized. But what ever occurs, whether in reference to God's providence for us or to the government and constitution of the universe, occurs through the three Persons, and is not three separate things.[47]

## The Cappadocians and the Spirit

Not only did Arianism force the fourth century church to clarify its teaching on the Father and Son, it also precipitated clarification regarding the Spirit. Whilst the threat from Sabellianism was met in asserting that the Spirit has his own 'way of being', the church's new task was to define both the status and identity of the Spirit over against the doctrine of the Trinity put forward by the Arians, namely of three infinitely dissimilar essences.[48]

It was from the unity perceived in any act of God that Basil attributed equal worship to the Father, Son and Spirit on the grounds that this indicates 'invariability of nature.'[49] However, he never went on to claim that the Spirit was God, or consubstantial, equal in substance, with the Father. This was to be developed by the two Gregories. Gregory of Nyssa asserted the particular identity of the Spirit: the Spirit receives his identity from the Father who is the cause of both the Son and the Spirit. The Spirit, consequently, receives his identity from the Father, through the Son.[50] Whilst Gregory does call the Spirit 'God' he never describes the Spirit as of the same substance, *homoousios*, as the Father. It was Gregory of Nazianzus who openly declared the consubstantiality of the Spirit with the Father, and in so doing, asserted the full divinity of the Spirit:

What then? Is the Spirit God? Most certainly. Well, then, is He Consubstantial? Yes, if He is God.[51]

The doctrine of God as Trinity now reached its zenith. In

true systematic form, Gregory of Nazianzus explained the late arrival of the Spirit's divinity on to the theological scene:

> The Old Testament proclaimed the Father openly, and the Son more obscurely. The New manifested the Son, and suggested the Deity of the Spirit. Now the Spirit Himself dwells among us and supplies us with a clearer demonstration of Himself. For it was not safe, when the Godhead of the Father was not yet acknowledged, plainly to proclaim the Son; nor when that of the Son was not yet received to burden us further . . . with the Holy Ghost.[52]

## A Progression in Thought

The ongoing task of trinitarian theology is rather like a mobile which moves according to the wind blowing against it. The content of such theology, like the mobile, remains constant and moves only insofar as it is required to answer the questions thrown up by each *Zeitgeist*, spirit of the age.[53] The Cappadocians facilitated a theological construction which expressed belief in a God who is both one and three by their use of the highly refined concepts of being and person. And so the development continues. At this point, then, we are able to return to Irving whose historical context is very far removed from that of the Cappadocians. Whilst it would be true to say that they all addressed a similar problem—theology, like history, does repeat itself—their method was somewhat different at points.

What is interesting to note is the fact that Irving, too, identifies God the Father in terms of monarchy and causality. He is the *fons trinitatis*, the source or cause from which the Son is begotten and the Spirit proceeds. The Father is the only one who is self-originated. And so, for Irving, the identity of the Father is the 'fundamental principle of the Trinity . . . His single prerogative, His precedency in being, though not in time'.[54] The Father's identity is derived from the fact that he has no origin, whilst the common attribute of self-existence shared by Father, Son and Spirit, safeguards the unity of the doctrine of the Trinity.

However, Irving does not stop here. He also identifies the Father in terms of will. The Father is the 'abysmal Will', the 'primary Founder' out of whom 'all things are and by whom we are'.[55] Throughout his argument Irving is at pains to safeguard against the notion that the grounds of being consist of an impersonal and unidentified will. The history of humanity is identified with God's history—the practical expression of a loving, paternal, not brute, will. In a later sermon, *The Theology of the Natural Man*, he argues against the Romantic notion of an intelligent Creator or superior Being derived from scientific observations of creation. This 'primary Founder' which Irving talks of is not to be identified with the idea of God as power of sovereignty, for such talk is insufficient to sustain the notion of a personal God. No provision is made in Irving's theology for the notion of a *vestigium trinitatis*, a natural trace of the Trinity.

> Now, supposing them to have made this step from the visible creation to an intelligent Creator, and that they did habitually, upon beholding nature, connect her forms and changes with a superior Being, they are still remote from any apprehension of the Christian's God, and incapable of those affections which we feel towards the God who is revealed in the Holy Scriptures. They have evidences of immeasurable power; but power doth not beget love . . . Whoever fastens upon God's attribute of sovereignty or power, and placeth that chiefly before his eyes, becomes a timorous devotee, a superstitious, feeble slave.[56]

The being of God as Father leads us to consider how Irving identifies the Son, and in particular, the ontical identity he ascribes to the Son, with God who is the ground of all being. We have noted that the Cappadocians identified the Son's particular manner of existing in terms of his being begotten of the Father. Irving, however, seeks to unpack the implications involved in talking of an eternal relationship between the Father and the Son. This he extrapolates from the Pauline notion that the Son is the very image of the Father. So Irving writes:

> Concerning the mystery of the eternal generation of the Son in the bosom of the Father, God forbid that I should speculate, or

even venture to think that I can comprehend it, or that I would liken it to anything in the heaven above or in the earth below. While I reverently contemplate it, and meditate upon it as a mystery of the Divine being hid within Himself, and receive it implicitly as a matter of divine faith, revealed for our knowledge of God, and comfort and delight in Him, all that I would attempt in discoursing thereof would be to shew unto His Church the streams of consolation and grace which flow from this most secret and mysterious fountain . . . The knowledge that the first act of the Godhead was to generate a Son in His own image and likeness, who should contain the fulness of Himself, and dwell within the object of all His delight, is such a proof of fellowship and communion and divine affection, as should fill every creature with trust and confidence, and assure our hearts before Him.[57]

What is of importance here is the manner in which Irving remains consistent with his own Scottish theological tradition, which Barth identifies as the balance between the 'majesty of God' and the 'person of God'.[58] The majesty of God remains an ultimate mystery: the human mind lacks capacity to comprehend the incomprehensible and infinite. However, Irving differs from the Eastern Fathers in that he resists any philosophical speculation in order to identify God's being. Secondly, and following on from this, is Irving's insistence that the Father chooses to reflect, or image, himself in and through his Son. The eternal generation of the Son, subsequently, is identified not with a bare, omnipotent will, but with the loving will of the Father. The Son's generation consists 'in His being, then, the object of all affection, and delight unto the Father before the world was.'[59]

Up to this point in his apologetic, Irving's use of both the fatherhood and eternal sonship of God reflects his dependence upon the theological tradition within which he trained. Only once does he suggest an element of independence which could be deemed specifically innovative. We have highlighted this as the means by which he arrives at his doctrine of the Trinity. Whereas the Cappadocians arrived at the Son's divine status through developing the available language, Irving pursues the same goal without such linguistic dexterity. Rather, he establishes the divine status of the Son in both soteriological and paternal terms. The One who comes to us in saving grace is also the bearer of the Father's grace. Therefore, there is an intimate connection between who Christ is and what he does, between his sonship and saving action.

If the Cappadocian defence was partly developed in isolation from explicitly soteriological, saving, implications, then Irving's is a complete reversal in theological method. The Cappadocians, despite their remonstrations to the contrary, treated data about God as primary data which could be treated as an object of investigation. Irving, however, consistently treats such data as secondary data contingent upon the context within which human beings find themselves.[60] God's trinitarian being is intimately associated with his saving action. Consequently, as we turn to consider the manner by which Irving delineates his understanding of God the Spirit in relation to that of Father and Son, we confront an innovation that moves away from the Cappadocian method to one that draws more heavily upon the specific relation of the Spirit.

## Irving and the Spirit

However much we may agree in sentiment with Mackey's remark that '*trinitarian* theology stands or falls with the doctrine of the Holy Spirit',[61] we must add that the degree to which this occurs is contingent upon the specific identity given to the Spirit. The doctrine of the Spirit remains the Achilles' heel of trinitarian thought. With Gregory of Nazianzus' triumph in systematizing Cappadocian thought, the Spirit's role in the divine economy came to be interpreted via fourth century theistic presuppositions.[62] Consequently, we take leave of our Cappadocian comparison and turn our attention to the first of Irving's major innovations within his own Western tradition.

The God who identifies himself as Father and Son is further identified as Spirit. But what does it mean to affirm God's being as Spirit? How do we understand God better through an understanding of his being Spirit? To what extent does it increase our knowledge of the transcendent and divine mystery? Perhaps here lies the hermeneutical problem of trinitarian theology. While we may be able to understand the relations of Father and Son, that of Spirit is more evasive in that it is much less self-explanatory. After all, we can imagine father and son in purely human terms: but what or who is spirit? It may not be too far from the mark to say that ecclesial and dogmatic histories repeat themselves in consistently succumbing to the danger of treating God the Spirit as both independent from and consequential to God the Father and Son. To various degrees, the Spirit has become an appendage to any trinitarian 'God-talk' and to this extent, Mackey's sentiment is correct.

In his attempt to solve the trinitarian problem, Irving does not remove God's being from the existential and practical needs of the church. Rather, he argues that our knowledge and articulation of God's being cannot be divorced from the Christian experience of God in Christ and the church. Therefore, the identity of the Spirit is not abstracted from what we understand of Christ alike in incarnation, salvation and Christian worship. However, Irving does not develop too total an identification of the economic Trinity with the immanent Trinity, that is God as he works both in creation and salvation with God as he is in himself as Father, Son and Spirit. Consistently, Irving holds to the belief that God's being remains ultimately a mystery. However, as stated earlier, this is not to say that God is mysterious in every respect. Our knowledge of God as Father, Son and Spirit is derived from God's gracious activity towards fallen humanity. To this degree, God's being is known in God's becoming—he makes himself known in his action towards us.[63]

How does Irving, then, help us here? What is of interest when we look at his understanding of God, is his lack of interest in any philosophical expression concerning the unity of God. Irving obviously adheres to what can be deemed monotheistic trinitarianism with its notion of the oneness of God's being. Although he alludes to the divine 'substance' it is, in fact, always at the background of his thinking. Irving's concern, rather, is with the personal relations between Father, Son and Spirit in incarnation and redemption. As a result, his doctrine of God as Trinity is less abstract than that of the Cappadocians since he elucidates his understanding of the Trinity from his understanding of the biblical text. His soteriological concerns press him to consider the threefold relations of God in incarnation. Consequently, he makes very little use of substance-language, preferring to pursue what is an explicitly relational or personal unity. The ultimate grounds of being are not defined by substantial categories, they are relational. *Deus est ens super ens* only as Father, Son and Spirit.

With the Cappadocians the unity of God came to be presented in terms somewhat removed from the biblical expression. The unity of God's being was expressed in mainly substantial terms, since the debate that raged was concerned, primarily, with establishing that the Son was of the same substance as the Father, and so consequently was the Spirit. Irving, however, is at pains to show that God's being is to be found in his manner of relating, and not merely in his subsisting. And for Irving, the manner of relating is specifically pneumatic—it specifically concerns the Spirit. The God who differentiates himself as Father and Son does so through his being as Spirit. Here we confront Irving's solution to the trinitarian problem. 'God-talk' is given a relational and, in particular, pneumatological solution.

Although we find in Irving's vocabulary the notion of 'substance' it assumes a quite different meaning from its traditional use: it denotes the common characteristics shared by Father, Son and Spirit, namely, grace, love, justice, omnipotence, mercy.

If any one ask a Christian what is the name of his God, he doth not answer well unless he say, 'The Father, and the Son, and the Holy Ghost.' And when in blessing we do say . . . 'The grace of our Lord Jesus Christ, the love of God the Father, and the communion of the Holy Ghost be with you all,' we use that word God in connexion with the Father, not to signify that He only is God, but to signify His Divine substance; just as for the same reason we use the title Lord Jesus Christ unto Jesus, and the title the Holy unto the Spirit.[64]

The task for Irving is to establish whether or not his response is capacious enough to state clearly a theological perspective which maintains a belief in the unity of Father, Son and Spirit. Irving's answer turns specifically on the belief that God's being is to be found in the manner of his relating, which he delineates in terms of the Father and the Son whose relation establishes and facilitates the notion of love. In so doing, he moves away from a purely Western perspective which tended to appropriate the title of Love to the Spirit. For instance, Augustine suggested that if any of the Trinity 'be specifically called love, what more fitting than that this should be the Holy Spirit . . . The Holy Spirit is specifically called love.'[65] In turn, Richard of St. Victor took the development further: the Spirit is that which represents the overflow of the love between the Father and the Son. The Spirit is realized as the one whose existence within the Trinity perfects the divine love.[66] What is of interest here is the fact that the identity of the Spirit is deduced more philosophically than it is biblically, for although Richard is at pains to develop a biblical perception of divine being as Love, the manner by which he attributes this to the Spirit reflects more his deductive presuppositions than scriptural exegesis.

When we turn to Irving, however, we discover that he does not apply the notion of love within the divine relations to the Spirit but to the Father and Son. In particular he refers to the Son as the one who is the image of the Father's loving will. Irving rejects the idea of identifying the Spirit as Love, on the grounds that 'we have no such expression as the Father loving the Holy Spirit, or the Son loving the Holy Spirit—the love being always from the Father to the Son and terminating in the Son.'[67]

How, then, does he identify God's being as Spirit? He continues the Eastern stress in identifying the Spirit in terms of procession, that is, the Spirit proceeds from the Father. At the same time he unpacks the implications involved in this assertion. Like generation, procession implies both 'the idea of the originating will of another, and self-existence (not creature-existence) in that which is originated.' Irving has used the idea of generation to imply 'the most perfect love in him who begetteth, and the most perfect likeness in him who is begotten.' However, because of his understanding of the gospel, Irving believed this expression fell short of the Christian experience of God, both in scriptural and personal terms. Thus he develops the complementary and necessary role the Spirit plays within the divine community. God's being as Spirit, as the one who proceeds, 'implies a full and fixed purpose in him from whom the procession is, and an active obedience and complete power of fulfilment in him who proceedeth.'[68] As such, the Spirit differs from the Father, who is self-originated, and from the Son, who is generated and images the Father's love. The Spirit, as we have noted earlier, is further distinguished from the Son in that it is only in the filial and paternal divine relations that we are introduced to God's love.

However, things are still rather dim. As God the Spirit is distinguished in the act of procession, there is no immediate analogy by which we can interpret his particular identity. Perhaps here we are confronted by the self-effacing identity of the Spirit—an implicit resistance to any thoroughly explicit identity. The Spirit is God's being in his 'otherness'.[69] The Spirit is both God's being-for-the-Other and God's being-to-the-Other. Therefore, from his understanding of the incarnation, Irving proposes the following identity of the Spirit. If the purpose of creation and redemption 'revealeth the activity and the power of the Holy Ghost to shew forth and outwardly realise . . . those correlative affections which existed in the Father and the Son, or, in Scripture language, to testify of the Father and the Son,' then 'this procession of the Holy Ghost from the Father and the Son, and love to manifest their being, must have been in existence before the purpose to reveal the same could be formed.'[70]

Thus far, Irving has not generated any significant development within his theological tradition. Where this does occur is at the point in which he attributes to the Spirit the means by which the Trinity is united as a community of beings. We have noted already that Irving accords personal, though not ontological, priority to the Father. Traditionally this *monarchia* has been accommodated alongside the equality of nature shared by Father, Son and Spirit. Consequently, we can almost say that it is natural for God to be relational. In the history of Western dogmatic expression, however, the nature of God tended to be the means by which God's unity was maintained. Irving moves away from this priority to develop a more personal and relational understanding of divine unity. Thus he argues:

> In the sublime exordium of the Gospel by John, it is said of the Word that He was with God, and that He was God, and that He came forth from the bosom of God: and in . . . Colossians, it is said that it pleased the Father that in Him all fulness should dwell: expressions these which convey in the strongest terms the diversity of persons in the Godhead, the subordination of place in the unity of substance, between these two, the Father and the Son. But this unity of substance between two divers persons can only be maintained, even in idea, by the existence of a third person, who shall be the bond of that union. If the Father in His own personality were to speak or to do anything to the Son to the end of his coming into the bounds of the Christ, or if He were to express or shew forth any affection to Him, in that subsistence, then doth the Father himself come within the limits thereof, and unlimitable infinite Godhead ceases to be the inalienable property of the Father.[71]

For Irving, the very unity of divine being demands more than two persons. In this sense, Irving parallels the logic of Richard of St. Victor, but differs in that whilst Richard argued for the Spirit's existence in order to establish the quality of divine love, Irving does so in order to clarify and establish the grounds of divine self-relating. If God's being is his self-relating, then it is a self-relating that operates in a specifically pneumatic manner, that is, it is held together by the Spirit.

> As the Father doth, in the primeval and one only complete act of His will, generate the Son, in whom are included, and through whom are operated, all the various particular acts

thereof; so from the Father and the Son, in their harmonious union, proceedeth the Holy Ghost; through whom, before creation, in the depths of eternity, the Son expresseth unto the Father the perfect unity of His being, notwithstanding that distinctness of personality which He had bestowed upon Him. The self-existence of the Son, and the self-existence of the Father would constitute them twain in existence, as well as in personality, *were it not for the procession of the Holy Ghost from both in whose self-existing intercommunion they behold, and are satisfied, with their oneness* . . . The Spirit being originated both from the Father and the Son, must in His self-existent being represent the unity and harmony of these two self-existent Beings.[72]

The unity of God's trinitarian being is communicated neither in any abstracted manner, nor in the relation between primary and secondary substance, nor by means of any psychological analogies derived from self-reflection. Rather, for Irving, the Achilles' heel of trinitarian theology becomes the very cornerstone to his entire ontology. It is a personal and thoroughly pneumatic union. The primacy of the Father's will in generating the Son is not that which causes the Spirit's procession. The Spirit proceeds *ex patre filioque*, both from the Father and the Son. On this point much could be said. Irving, as usual, defies categories. On the one hand, he talks of the Spirit proceeding from the Father *and* the Son. At other points, he talks of the Spirit proceeding from the Father *through* the Son. Irving takes the *filioque* most seriously because of its givenness within the Christian story. What we know of the Spirit is that which we 'encounter' in divine revelation, in particular as it is seen in the Spirit's relationship to Christ in incarnation.

By going forth to set on foot any mighty work, and creating the elemental life of it, He doth thereby, in working his own personal and distinct work, so far forth express their unity and oneness of substance; while by staying at a certain point, and confessing His inability to proceed further, He doth give honour to the superior place, and room for the independent self-sufficiency of the Son who now cometh forth, whether as Word, or as the only-begotten Son (for He is both from all eternity in

His very substance), to give forms, and functions, and laws of being yet all the while declaring that He can work nothing by Himself, nor put will into anything, being Himself but the great offspring of the Father's will, for the decree of which every work waiteth, and without which no work of the Godhead is complete. And the work being complete doth acknowledge the origination of its life to the Spirit, the excellent form and peculiar blessedness of its life to the Son, the end and continual support of its life to the Father's will.[73]

Who is God? He is the one who reveals himself through his being-for-others. Or as Barth puts it, 'The reality of God which encounters us in His revelation is his reality in all the depths of eternity.'[74] For Irving, the way in which God acts in history in order to reconcile human beings to himself, reveals to us the true identity of God. The way in which we identify God's being as Spirit in the incarnation, reveals the very unity of God's being-for-himself. And who is the Spirit? He is, like the Son, identified in terms of his relations both to the Father and the Son. Consequently, for Irving, the Spirit is both *ex patre*, from the Father, and *filioque*, the Son.

Perhaps Irving is trying to have his ecumenical cake and eat it, but it is clear that he holds to both the procession of the Spirit as coming from the Father alone, and from the Father and the Son. In so doing, he appears to understand the ultimate grounds of being to be interrelated and interpersonal. It is the essential union between Father, Son and Spirit which gives meaning to the term person. It is a meaning derived from the work of God the Trinity in the incarnation. Thus, the trinitarian and christological meaning of person reveals to us what it means to be truly a person, not the other way round: the term person owes its meaning to christology in its 'metaphysical foundation.'[75] To be a person is to be in relation as interdependent not independent.

So Irving develops somewhat dormant theological threads within his own trinitarian tradition. However, it is not a unique development the quest of establishing the identity of the Spirit took on an earlier innovation under the Cappadocian fathers. How did they solve this problem?

Basil argued that the Spirit is not a creation of the Father nor of a different nature from the Father. Anastos points out that Basil insisted that, 'the Holy Spirit has a kinship with the Father and Son . . . that the Spirit is holy, good, a bestower of special spiritual gifts (such as sonship of God and the immortality of the body), and one which shares in divinity.' However, Basil found it difficult to state explicitly that the Spirit is *God*.[76] Thus, Basil himself states that the Council of Nicea deferred comment because 'at the time of the Council, no question was mooted, and the opinion of this subject in the hearts of the faithful was exposed no attack.'[77] It was the threat from Arianism, that the Son is a creature, that brought this to the foreground. Basil, however, remains silent on a pronouncement concerning the divine status of the Spirit: a considerably significant silence reflecting biblical and theological humility on Basil's part.

Whilst Gregory of Nazianzus defends Basil's silence on the grounds of his desire not to alienate the wavering[78] as well as on technical grounds, affirming that Basil's terminology is not to be considered as 'the utmost limit of truth'[79] more modern scholars vary in their testimony to Basil. Meredith argues negatively that Basil's caution in ascribing equal honour to the Spirit is not an 'eirenic gesture' nor an example of his 'economy', but due to his 'imperfect (or barely existent) awareness of the role played by the Holy Spirit in the work of creation.'[80]

Perhaps this is overly critical. We must remember that explicit doctrines had not yet been established. Much was still to be discussed. In addition, despite the philosophical background to his thought, Basil does reflect the same caution reflected in the New Testament regarding the identity of the enigmatic Spirit. Such is the task given the theologian: his original context (in Basil's case, the New Testament) and the contemporary context (a fragile church) meant that he had to articulate his response within the given boundaries. Therefore, he withstood the pressure to affirm any explicit statements about the Spirit's divinity although the substance of his writings suggests the Spirit to be God. In addition, as Zizioulas points out, Basil was following the Cappadocian line of argument: substance-language was only used when comparing God with the world. That is, God is one substance, creation is another. It was used in the Father-Son debate to indicate that the Son is not a creature but God, the same substance as God. Basil, then, did not use this language because it was not relevant to the issues being raised about the Spirit.[81]

In *Being as Communion*, Zizioulas argues for a particular interpretation of Cappadocian ontology. He argues that Basil, in re-defining 'person' introduces a new philosophical concept: a fact the history of philosophy has not noted. No longer is 'substance' the ultimate principle of being this ultimacy is now accorded to 'person'. For the Cappadocians, the ultimate ontological principle becomes 'person', and specifically the Person of the Father, who causes, by a free act of his being, both the Son and the Spirit. Consequently, the Trinity is not derived from a substance, but from a person, the Father. 'What therefore is important in trinitarian theology is that God 'exists' on account of a person, the Father, and not on account of a substance.'[82] From this person, by a free and personal act, are caused the Son and the Spirit. The Father becomes the cause of the Persons of the Trinity and as such, the being of God resides in communion with the Father, not a divine substance. 'Communion arises from the person of the Father, not the substance of God. It is the Father as divine person, and not the divine nature that is ecstatic.'[83]

Zizioulas' interpretation is both illuminating and refreshing, and possibly permissible within an Orthodox hermeneutic, wherein he can be better interpreted as expanding upon the tradition he inherits. However, is his a fair presentation of what the Cappadocians themselves argued? It would appear not, for they held in tension both the substantial and the personal, doing so in order to refute both Sabellianism and Arianism as well as its extreme form, Eunomianism, which identified the substance of God with the Father, and attributed a lower from of existence to the Son. To reject the efficacy of substance-language in their own method, is to undermine a bulwark established by them in order to defend rational talk of God as a Trinity of Persons against these misrepresentations of the Christian doctrine of God. It would appear that for them, the substance of God is a fundamental category within their ontology.

Secondly, all three Cappadocians argue quite unequivocally for a communion of divine substance, not persons, as Zizioulas argues. Rather, Basil states that,

> in the case of the Godhead, we confess one *ousia* or substance so as not to give a variant definition of existence.[84]

Indeed, Basil appears to make the point very clear that any notion of causality is to be located within the notion of *hypostasis*:

> But God, Who is over all, alone has, as one special mark of His own *hypostasis*, His being Father, and His deriving His *hypostasis* from no cause; and through this mark He is peculiarly known.[85]

Thirdly, Gregory of Nyssa argues for a distinction in person and nature vis-à-vis causality:

> Although we acknowledge the nature is undifferentiated, we do not deny a distinction with respect to causality. That is the only way by which we distinguish one Person from the other, but believing . . . that one is the cause and the other depends on the cause . . . When we speak of a cause and that which depends on it, we do not, by these words refer to nature. For no one would hold that cause and nature are identical.[86]

It is because all three, Father, Son and Spirit, fully possess the one divine nature, that the Cappadocians could safely talk of a *monarchia* and a causality from the Father, without inferring any ontological subordination.

When we compare the Cappadocian response, the hitherto greatest theological expression of divine being, with that of Irving, we find both similarities and differences. On the one hand, Irving's interest in and stress on the divine relations parallels that which we see in the Cappadocians, and whilst it can hardly be said that such a stress is missing in Western theology,[87] Irving's emphasis appears to be much more at home within the theological tradition expressed both by Cappadocian thought and its progression in Ziziou-las.

However, on the other hand, Irving's doctrine of God differs significantly and specifically from the Cappadocians' by virtue of its pneumatic dimension. The Cappadocians developed language in order to establish the specific identity of the Spirit: the Spirit is divine not so much in terms of what he does in the economy and thereby displaying who he is, as in terms of him being the same substance as God the Father.

Irving, however, differs in method and in identifying this difference we are better equipped to understand the significance of Irving's contribution to the trinitarian problematic. He refuses to acknowledge a radical distinction between the reality of God's being-for-himself and that reality which can be seen in his action for others. The Cappadocians maintained a clear distinction between the two by means of their apophatic theology that is, the otherness of God is so great that he can only be described in terms of what he is *not*. Irving argues the reverse. God's being is understood from the perspective of the 'event', the incarnation, wherein is highlighted the Spirit's relation to the Father and the Son. It is, therefore, from the event of incarnation that Irving delineates his understanding of the divine relations. Irving would agree with later theologians that God is finally a mystery 'hid within Himself' which is revealed through the incarnation in such a way that 'God reveals himself as Father, Son and Spirit because he *is* Father, Son and Spirit.'[88] And for Irving, he does so in such a manner as to reveal that the Spirit is the *vinculum unitatis*, the uniting link within the Trinity. The Father is Father because of the Son, and vice-versa, but both are incomprehensible in their trinitarian being apart from the Spirit, who, in turn, is understood only in his specific relation with the Father and the Son.

Nevertheless, God is no object of theoretical speculation: theological talk of God remains iconic, or what Polanyi calls, 'inarticulate' knowledge.[89] Although knowledge of divine being is derived from the perspective of incarnation, this knowledge is something given. Our knowledge of God's being both for himself and for others, comes to us by grace:

that which he has done in and through Jesus Christ.
Consequently, although Irving proceeds with caution, this
does not imply we are left to grope in the dark in a confused
and meaningless manner. He insists upon a clear distinction
between the subject of revelation and the means of revelation. Our knowledge about God is not derived from any
state of human self-consciousness, but from the transcendent moment in human history when the divine became
enfleshed within time. In addition our knowledge of this is
not natural. It is thoroughly pneumatological. Thus the community of the faithful invoke *'Per te sciamus de PATREM
noscamus atque FILIUM Te UTRISQUE SPIRITUM
credamus omni tempore*. Grant that we may know the
Father and the Son through Thee; and that we may believe
Thee, the Spirit of both at all times.'

## The Means of Grace

> Only one, Eternal,
>   all pervading one,
>     invisible,
>   and indefinable God!
>
> Other gods are but inventions,
>   within the minds of men.
> In whom the Almighty one cannot be
>   contained.
>
> Can he never be seen?
>   Is he never visible?
> Why? Can your almighty God
>   not reveal himself before us?[90]

The question of God's being, his existence and identity is
surely as problematic now, as it was for Schœnberg's Moses.
If God is 'indefinable because invisible, and unobservable,
and unbounded, and eternal, and all pervading,'[91] then is
not all 'God-talk' merely the Cheshire cat of ingenious
theology? Are we not forced to halt at the final words
attributed by Schœnberg to Moses?

And all was but madness
that I believed before,
which can and must not be spoken of!
O Word
That Word, which I am denied.[92]

There has never been a more succinct Christian reply to this predicament than that given by St John in his prologue: this Word became flesh. It is he who expresses the unspoken Word. This is no *Deus absconditus*, no absent God. Rather, herein is the *Deus revelatus*, the God who reveals himself. 'No one has ever seen God: the only Son, who is in the bosom of the Father, he has made him known.'[93] The silence suggested by Schœnberg's Moses is shattered by divine fiat. The Johannine Son diffuses the darkness with dawning light. The indefinable, unobservable, unbounded and eternal becomes known in the Son. By no other means do we comprehend the infinite and eternal. This fundamental element of Johannine theology becomes the foundation for Irving's entire ontology. Undergirding his entire doctrine of God is the belief that, 'through Christ, and Christ only, who is the Godhead in a body, could the Godhead out of a body, the infinite and invisible Godhead, ever have been known. . . . God is known by His acts . . . We come by the knowledge of the invisible Godhead of the Father, through the visible Godhead of the Son'.[94]

However, Irving has argued already that God's creative action alone cannot reveal any knowledge of a personal God. If this were so, we could deduce the unity of God's being in a manner similar to that which Irving opposed in the Unitarians and Deists. Consequently, although there was little doubt over the unity of God's being within the church, Irving maintains a very clear distinction between the unity held by the church and that propounded by his secular contemporaries. As he puts it, theirs is a false God, a certain idea of perfect being and infinite power which they have from their own brain, an abstraction of certain properties of man, a generalization of certain principles of matter, 'a great first cause least understood, an all-pervading power, and everything or anything but the true, self-existing, personal God'.[95]

Nevertheless, the pressing problem lies not so much with the question of monotheism but with the means by which we maintain trinitarian monotheism. There is no doubt in Irving's mind that outside of the New Testament there is no knowledge of a trinity of persons in the God. There is no question of a *vestigium trinitatis*, a vestige or remnant of the Trinity. We have absolutely no knowledge of a trinitarian deity outside the revelation in Christ. At this point we confront the christocentric nature of Irving's entire thought: knowledge of God as Father, Son and Spirit, is derived solely from the history and person of Jesus Christ. Irving's, then, is a supremely christocentric hermeneutic. God's self-identity as Father, Son and Spirit is only known as such, *pro nobis*, because of his visible and historical being-for-others as Son, a point continually unpacked by Irving at every possible point.

> It was not until the Son came into manifestation as a man, until the Word was made flesh and dwelt among us, became our Saviour, the long-expected Messiah on earth, the long-looked for Christ and Lord in heaven, for whom all things were created, that the truth of the glorious Trinity became a grand and manifest truth for ever. Because so soon as the Son became manifest He made known the Father, to whom He always inferred back as the eternal Father of the Son, and in Him the great originator of all things, and principal party to the eternal purpose which the Son came forth to reveal. 'No one has ever seen God: the only Son, who is in the bosom of the Father, he has made him known.' By the same act also did the Spirit become manifest; for . . . Christ's becoming outward and visible was the act of the Spirit.[96]

It is in his searing criticism of his opponents that Irving reveals the full import he accords the incarnation in making known to us the character of the triune God. It is when he turns upon his Unitarian and Socinian opponents that we are most privy to the magisterial position he gives to the person and work of Christ.

> Ye may be able to state out the redemption, without a Trinity of persons in the Godhead: I lay claim to no such ability. Your

Trinity is an idle letter in your creed; but it is the soul, the life of mine. Your Christ is a suffering God; I know it well: my Christ is a gracious condescending God, but a suffering man. In your Christ, you see but one person in a body: in my Christ I see the fulness of the Godhead in a body. My Christ is the Trinity manifested not merely the Trinity told of, but the Trinity manifested. I have the Father manifested in everything which He doth; for he did not His own will, but the will of His Father. I have the Son manifested, in uniting His Divinity to a humanity prepared for Him by the Father; and in making the two most contrary things to meet and kiss each other, in all the actings of his widest, most comprehensive being. I have the Holy Ghost manifested in subduing, restraining, conquering, the evil propensities of the fallen manhood, and making it an apt organ for expressing the will of the Father, a fit and holy substance to enter into personal union with the untempted and untemptable Godhead.[97]

Such is the emphasis Irving places upon the doctrines of Christ and the Trinity. They are intimately united, since for him the act of God in incarnation reveals the being of God in himself, and the former for Irving is clearly trinitarian. It is because the Christ is the eternal Son that Irving must relate his doctrine of God as Trinity to everything he states about Christ. It is only through an understanding of the relation between the two in general, and between the Father and the Son in particular, that we then gain insight into Irving's understanding of the Spirit. In this sense, Irving's method follows the line of argument assumed by the Fathers: only once the debate about the Son had been resolved, could questions about the Spirit be addressed. The questions determine the ultimate response. For Irving, these questions were unequivocally important.

Irving's response to the christological, and therefore trinitarian, challenges coming from Unitarian thinking shaped his major polemic. His primary thrust of argument rests on establishing the eternal status of the Son. We can identify three different threads to his argument.

Firstly, he wishes to identify the Father with the name 'God'. For Irving, knowledge of God's being as Father is derived solely from the incarnation. Before the act of incarnation when in his procession from the Father the Son 'took unto Himself flesh of the Virgin Mary'[98] the name 'God' denoted only 'the supreme unity and majesty of the Godhead, without any reference simply to the specialities of His revelations.'[99] It was only 'when the time came to open the mystery of the Trinity', that 'this name of God received a special and particular application to the Father'.[100] Any mention of God before this event is to be attributed to the 'Godhead in its unity' where the substance of the Godhead is represented 'without any respect to the personalities thereof'.[101] The term 'God' belongs, then, to the first person of the Trinity designating 'His essential Godhead and His self-origination, as distinguished from the Son and the Holy Ghost, whose prerogative it is only to be self-existent'.[102]

Secondly, the means by which Irving establishes the union between the eternal Son and Jesus Christ is more protracted, being approached from a double angle. The first is tackled at the start of his Trinity sermons. Irving raises it in the form of a question: If the Greek form 'God' is distinct from the Hebrew LORD, and the identity of the former remains unknown until the event of incarnation, then who is made known to us in the Old Testament? If the Father at all times remains invisible, being known only through the visible manifestation of the Son, then who is the subject of divine revelation in the history of Israel? For Irving, the incarnation is not a totally unique event in salvation history since he identifies the second person of the Trinity with the Old Testament appellations, 'LORD' and 'Jehovah'. Irving identifies the Old Testament title 'LORD' with that of 'Lord' in the New Testament by means of Acts 2:36, 'Therefore let all the house of Israel know assuredly, that God hath made that same Jesus, whom ye crucified, both Lord and Christ,' the last two titles being interpreted as 'Jehovah' and 'Anointed One'. Consequently, 'this title of "The Lord" is . . . appropriate to Christ . . . It belongs to the second person of the Trinity by special inheritance, and not to the Godhead in its revealed and undivided essence, for which the proper name is God'.[103]

Thirdly, having established a union between these names,

Irving turns his attention to the specific manner by which Jesus Christ may be identified as God the Son. In order to do so, he resorts to a somewhat complicated hermeneutic. He identifies the name 'Jesus' as *Jehoshua*. 'Jah' signifies a contraction of the divine name, 'Jehovah' found in Psalm 118:4 where it denotes the full force of the name. Elsewhere, 'Jah' denotes the eternal signature revealed to Moses in Exodus 3:14, 'I AM THAT I AM', teaching us 'that self-existent, underived, unchangeable, self-sufficient being is that which is contained under the name Jehovah.'[104] Finally, the name 'Jehovah', or its compound 'Jah', has been compounded into the name 'Jesus', who in Revelation 1:8 identifies himself in similar terms, 'I am Alpha and Omega, the beginning and the end . . . which is, and which was, and which is to come, the Almighty.'

In addition, Irving unpacks the significance of 'Hoshea' to mean 'Saviour' or 'salvation'. 'Hoshea' or 'Saviour' amplifies the identity of the former 'Jehovah'. Under the old Covenant, 'Jehovah' is known only as Judge: 'It is manifest from God's revealing Himself as Jesus, or the Saviour, that the creatures are in a state of condemnation . . . otherwise what meaning were there in revealing Himself as their Saviour?'[105] Conversely, by means of his appellation, 'Hoshea', he who formerly is identified as Judge, by becoming the incarnate one and assuming the name 'Jesus', identifies himself as Saviour.

Inasmuch as God's being is revealed through his personal action, Irving reaches the point wherein he identifies God's being as Son with the history and person of Jesus.

That word, Jah, incorporated with Hoshea in the name of our blessed Lord, is to me a pledge that all things which are written in the law and the prophets the Son of man hath come not to destroy but to fulfil. And accordingly we do find that Jesus hath applied to Him the essential meaning of Jehovah, which is independence on all outward causes, and unalterable by time . . . Unto this much have we attained, therefore, that all the might and holiness, all the magnificence of power and splendour of operation, all the faithfulness and immovableness of purpose, together with all words whatsoever written of Jehovah and the old dispensation, are the property of Him who hath revealed

Himself under the new as a man of sorrows and acquainted with grief, the meek, the humble, and the lowly Jesus.[10]

By doing this, Irving identifies God's being with the subject of the incarnation, Jesus. His defence, however, is not entirely complete. Irving has introduced us to the premiss that the divine is revealed in personal event. There is purpose to such activity: its underlying reason is neither capricious nor indiscriminate. God's being-for-others reveals an essential order of relatedness which not only pervades the entire event of incarnation, but can be traced back to the very ground of being itself, the Trinity of Father, Son and Spirit.

God's being, according to Irving, is in his relating. The essential character of God cannot be understood except in an essentially trinitarian fashion. We should not under-estimate the importance Irving accords his doctrine of God in the fight against current Unitarian arguments. God's being is in his self-relating as Father, Son and Spirit. Therefore, the doctrine of God is, at best, an attempt to harmonize the differing relations and functions of Father, Son and Spirit. In turn, every subsequent doctrine implicitly revolves around a threefold premiss Irving brings to every theological discussion. Each aspect of divine truth is pitted against three criteria:

as it is in the eternal being and purpose of God;
as it is manifested to us in the revelation of God; . . .
as it is applied to and appropriated by us for our promotion in the favour of God.[107]

To focus solely upon the first, he elucidates, leads only to fatalism and quietism, wherein we either 'are blinded by the darkness of too much light, or lost in the insignificancy of our own being'.[108] Alternatively, if we focus on the revelation in Christ without applying it to the Father's purposes, it can lead only to ignorance about the human will, namely that we 'either forget that man hath a will, or believe that the will is determined by the conviction of the mind on the affections of the heart'.[109] Lastly, if our attention is given only to the experiential, then 'it very speedily introduceth an ignorant, coarse, and homely way of religion, which never elevates the soul from its natural grovelling'.[110] In these, Irving argues, we see the respective dangers of Calvinism, Arminianism and Evangelicalism.

## The Means of Grace and Personal Will

God's being is in his relating, that is, he is personal event: he reveals himself, not things about himself, in the event of relating. The great mystery revealed in his activity is that a 'trinity of persons' is revealed in God's being-for-others: 'not a thought, nor a word,' but being-in-action.[111]

> The Divinity follows out its eternal and necessary law of being in the secret recesses of its own harmonious purpose, with which no creature intermeddleth, and of which no creature is competent to discourse, further than to say, 'Thus it is, because it is revealed that there is a trinity of persons in the Godhead'.[112]

Not only does the incarnation reveal to us the content of God, namely, that there is indeed a trinity of persons in the Godhead, it also reveals to us the form of God, that is, the manner by which this trinity of persons exists. It reveals to us a Father who at all times remains hidden, a Son who chooses to make the Father known, and a Spirit who both unites the Father and Son, and brings to fruition the act of the Son's revelation.

At this point we are now able to unpack the means by which Irving understands the incarnation to open up more fully the character of the trinitarian God.

In order to avoid the danger of aimless drifting, trinitarian theology, for Irving, must be grounded in the event of incarnation. To do so, Irving must establish an intimate connection between Christ's identity as Word and that of Son, as we noted earlier. As Word he reveals what has been spoken 'before the beginning of the world' and by doing so proves that 'a revelation by word is older than the fountain-head of time, even as old as the purpose of the Ancient of Days.'[113] It is only because Christ is the Father's Word, that the Son who dwells in the bosom of the Father is able to reveal the Father whom he alone knows. The Wisdom of God is thoroughly relational—he is Son.

> The word is not uttered by the invisible Father, who speaketh nothing but by the Son; nor is it spoken by the Holy Ghost, who speaketh nothing which He hath not heard of the Son; but is spoken by the Son, who speaketh nothing of Himself, but what He heareth from the Father. Neither by the Son is it spoken in His infinite Godhead, but in His predestined creature form.[114]

But how does the enfleshed Word communicate the purpose of the Father? Through the Spirit. Not only is the Spirit is *vinculum unitatis*, the uniting bond, he is also understood by Irving as '*vinculum trinitatis*, the circle of communication between the Father and Son.'[115]

The independence of Irving's thought is highlighted here in this most central of ideas. As noted, traditionally, the Spirit's specific role within the divine relations has been presented in agapeic terms, that is, as the one by whom the love of the Father for the Son and that of the Son for the Father is fulfilled. Irving's doctrine of God, however, prohibits any ascription of love to the Spirit. His pneumatology, rather, turns on the notion of energies: the Spirit includes within himself every possible activity of God. Of course, this is not to suggest any divorce between divine being and divine action. The Spirit cannot be understood as the energy of God in a way similar to diesel in an engine. To do so would be to annul any meaningful talk of revelation as well as to fall into the perpetual mistake of Western theology in perceiving the Spirit in material terms. For Irving, there is no ontological difference between the divine essence and its energies. If there is a difference, it can only be an epistemological one based on the fact that we are created and therefore limited in our understanding due to our finite capacities.[116]

Perhaps here we catch a glimpse of the influence on Irving of one of his greatest mentors, Samuel Taylor Coleridge, who remarked that 'the question of the nature of the real was not simply a pragmatic one about its operation: the real had to be seen in its connection to its foundation'[117] Therefore, when Irving attests that the incarnate Word reveals the Father's purpose and will which is completed by the energizing of the Spirit, we are not to interpret this in any other manner than that the divine activity seen in incarnation and redemption is not only consistent with, but reveals the very character of God.

In this we confront the primary thrust of Irving's thought: the incarnation is God's event. And because it is God's event it is capable of revealing God, not just things about God, but God himself. Thus, for Irving, the incarnating event is the revealing event, and, as such, is the trinitarian event.

Undergirding his entire thought, here, is the absolute primacy he attributes to will. The purpose of the incarnation is, *ipso facto*, to reveal God's will. And since God's will is consonant with this very being, knowledge of the will of God reveals the very being of God.

> It is the great purpose of the Divine will which God was minded from all eternity to make known unto His creatures, for their greater information, delight and blessedness, to make known . . . to all His intelligent creatures the grace and mercy, the forgiveness and love which he beareth towards those who love the honour of His Son, and believe in the word of His testimony.[118]

This personal will is reaffirmed in the act of incarnation. How? In the fact that it is, in many ways, the recapitulation of God's will for his creation. The Creator fulfils his personal will through being the Redeemer. Through the act of incarnation the Father reveals 'that more tender aspect of His being called *grace*—that part of the Divine substance which could not otherwise have been made known'.[119] This the Father achieves through the Son. The Son reveals this grace to us by revealing the Father, by 'setting forth every word as proceeding from the Father's will, and every act as the demonstration of His power.' Irving identifies this will in terms of purpose, that is the manifestation of the Son, and operation, that is the work of the Holy Spirit.[120] The really important point here is the trinitarian statement Irving makes concerning the Father's will: it is revealed in the Son through the Spirit. To this extent we have an insight into what Irving means when he holds to the belief that the Spirit proceeds from the Father and the Son. It would appear that he really believes that the Spirit proceeds from the Father *through* the Son. The Spirit is '*vinculum trinitatis*, the circle of communication between the Father and Son, through whom the will of the Father expresseth itself to the Son, and the obedience of the Son expresseth itself back again to the Father.'[121] Notice the intimacy Irving establishes here between the Father, Son and Spirit. Although the Father is ultimate Will, he chooses to work through the Son, whose role it is 'to word what the Father hath willed'[122] In turn, both unity and energy are established through the Spirit. If the Son performs what the Father wills, if the divine purpose is expressed in filial obedience, it is only the Spirit who brings into existence the fruit of cooperation between Father and Son. We have, of course, moved in consideration from divine being to divine activity. Nevertheless, this is consistent with Irving's method, where a distinction is made always between the two. The point to be stressed, which has been omitted by subsequent commentators, is the role Irving accords the Spirit. If God's being-for-himself as Father, Son and Spirit, is understood by means of his activity in salvation, then our supreme insight is derived from the event of incarnation, wherein 'cometh the knowledge of the three subsistencies in the Godhead, and of their common substance, what its purpose is, what its word is, and what its act is,' namely, Father, Son and Spirit.[123] Furthermore, it is from this revelation that we comprehend God in terms of personal Will residing in the Father, being revealed to us by the Son, but at all times accomplished through the Spirit who brings the Father's will and the Son's word into existence.[124]

This is no addendum or appendage to a primarily binitarian doctrine of God where the Father and the Son are clearly divine and the Spirit added as an afterthought. Rather, for Irving, the manner in which he identifies the Spirit reflects a thoroughgoing order of relatedness in which the Spirit is unequivocally God to the extent that God cannot *be* without the Spirit. Only by the presence and relatedness of all three, Father, Son and Spirit, is there a meaningful expression of the Christian God.

What, then, does Irving mean when he talks of God's being-for-himself in terms of personal Will? Is he not reducing his understanding of God to an impersonal concept? Perhaps not: Irving's mentor, Coleridge, argued for a thoroughgoing ontology of Will where 'the Triune God is, above all, Absolute Will'.[125] Coleridge argued for an understanding of the Trinity in which the notion of Will was aligned with that of Word and Love. Thus, he argued that, 'The Trinity is, 1. The Will; 2. The Reason or Word; 3. The Love, or Life. As we distinguish these three, so we must unite them in one God. The union must be as transcendent as the distinction'.[126]

The priority given by Coleridge in identifying God as Absolute and Personal Will both parallels and differs from that outlined by Irving. Firstly, we can trace Coleridge's influence on Irving in the stress on identifying the Father as Self-originating Will. If God is understood in terms of Will and this Will is identified with the Father, then it means that we are not dealing with an impersonal or abstract notion. Rather, we are dealing with an eternally personal reality, that is, the one who is Father from all eternity. This idea is only reinforced when we remember the manner in which Irving connects the impersonal Word with the personal Son.

Secondly, like Irving, Coleridge identifies the Spirit as 'the act, in which the Father and the Son are One'.[127] In a manner which Irving later re-echoes in his idea of the Spirit as *vinculum trinitatis*, Coleridge identifies the Spirit as the 'perfect Idea', as:

that which proceedeth from the Father to the Son, and that which is returned from the Son to the Father, and which in this circulation constitutes the eternal unity in the eternal . . . distinction, the life of Deity in *actus purissimu*. This is truly the Breath of life indeed, the perpetual action of the act, the perfect intellection alike of the *Intellectus* and of the Intelligible and the perpetual being and existing of that which saith 'I Am'.[128]

Where Irving parts company from Coleridge, is in Coleridge's perception of the Spirit as Act in purely agapeic terms. For Coleridge, it is a union of love: Love is the Spirit of God. As noted earlier, Irving clearly assigns the ascription of love to the Son, not the Spirit.

In conclusion then, we catch a glimpse of the route taken by Irving in arriving at his specific understanding of the Spirit. On the basis of Personal Will, Irving establishes a christology which gives a central place to the work and person of the Spirit. In that the Father's will is communicated to the Son, and the Son's obedience to the Father by means of the Spirit, and it comes as no surprise to discover a radical interpretation of the patristic maxim, *opera trinitatis ad extra indivisa sunt*. The external operations of the Trinity are indivisible because God is Trinity and therefore Father, Son and Spirit are indivisible in all they do, although not all do the same thing. This will be treated in Part III below. However, in order for us to understand Irving, we need first to turn our attention to an equally important but relatively unexplored dimension of his christology, namely his doctrine of human being. Whilst we have focused in this chapter on Irving's understanding of the trinitarian character of God, and in particular the relation of God the Spirit to the Father and Son, we now turn our attention to Irving's understanding of human being and the manner by which he is able to talk meaningfully about the Spirit's place in incarnation.

## Footnotes

[1] T Wolfe, *Of Time and the River. A Legend of Man's Hunger in His Youth*, New York: Charles Scribners' Sons, 1952, 34.
[2] Comment in J O'Donnell, 'The Trinity as Divine Community', *Gregoranium* 69.1, 1988, 5–34, 11–13.
[3] D Cupitt, *After All*, London: SCM Press Ltd, 1994, 42.
[4] John 1:1–3,14,17.
[5] AE Johnson, 'Christology's Impact on the Doctrine of God', *Heythrop Journal* XXVI (1985), 143–163, 145.
[6] The title of CE Gunton's 1992 Bampton Lectures, *The One, The Three and The Many*, Cambridge: CUP, 1993.
[7] Even theologians as different as Schleiermacher and Barth agree on

this point. See FDE Schleiermacher, *The Christian Faith*, Edinburgh: T & T Clark, 1986, §170, 738, and K Barth, *Church Dogmatics* 1.1, Edinburgh: T & T Clark, 1980, §8, 308.

[8] Basil of Caeserea, *Letters* NPNF[2] vol.VIII, Michigan: Wm.B.Eerdmans Publishing Company, 1975, CLXXXIX.6, 231.

[9] BB Warfield, *Calvin and Calvinism*, Hew York: OUP, 1931, 195.

[10] FDE Schleiermacher, op cit, 16ff, 18. Our interest in Schleiermacher will be expanded in detail in Part III. ST Coleridge, *Aids to Reflection*, Edinburgh: John Grant, MCMV, esp. 114: 'Aphorisms on that which is indeed spiritual religion.' Although Coleridge moves towards a trinitarian understanding of divine being, it is not as fully developed and therefore as integral to his theology as it is for Irving.

In addition, it is of interest to note Irving's contemporaneity with both scholars. Irving died in 1834, the same year as Coleridge and Schleiermacher, three years after Hegel, and two after Goethe.

[11] CW5, 350–351.

[12] TR Martland, 'A Study of Cappadocian and Augustinian Trinitarian Methodology', *Anglican Theological Review*, vol.47, 1965, 252–263, 252–253.

[13] MOW Oliphant, *Edward Irving*, London: Hurst and Blackett, 5th ed. no date, 220.

[14] Irving was excommunicated from the Church of Scotland on 13th March, 1833, at Annan, Scotland.

[15] See M Heidegger, *Being and Time*, London: SCM Press Ltd, 1962, 91.

[16] CW4, 223.

[17] CW4, 224–225.

[18] J Pelikan, *The Emergence of the Catholic Tradition (100–600)*, Chicago: The University of Chicago Press, 1971, 172.

[19] CW4, 228.

[20] CW4, 252.

[21] See Athanasius, *The Incarnation of the Word of God*, London: Geoffry Bles, 1944.

[22] L Carroll, *Alice's Adventures in Wonderland, and Through the Looking Glass*, London: JM Dent & Sons Ltd, 1981, 185–186.

[23] CW4, 245.

[24] CW4, 241–242.

[25] This similar line of thought is taken by John McLeod Campbell. Like Irving he was excommunicated from the Church of Scotland for teaching thought to be contrary to that of scripture and the Reformers. In McLeod Campbell's case, it was over the universal nature of God's love, rather than a particular love for the elect alone. Both he and Irving are adamant in their proclamation that in the work and person of Jesus Christ there is the full manifestation of the loving character of God. 'In the life of Christ, as the revelation of the Father by the Son, we see the love of God to man—the will of God for man—the eternal life which the Father has given to us in the Son.' *The Nature of Atonement*, London: James Clark and Co Ltd., 1949, 176.

[26] CW4, 246.

27 CW4, 258.

28 CW4, 258–259.

29 The most magisterial of which is Barth's *Church Dogmatics*, *supra*.

30 CW4, 259.

31 *ibid*

32 CW4, 260.

33 CW4, 261.

34 CW4, 262.

35 CW4, 261–262.

36 JG McGraw, 'God and the Problem of Loneliness', *Rel. Stud*, 28, 1993, 319–346.

37 See C Keisling, 'On Relating to the Persons of the Trinity', *Theological Studies*, 47, 1986, 599–616. The use of 'person' must carry some definite reality which embraces both its meaning for human beings and God. Despite the problems in using the term 'person' today vis-à-vis God, the word carries within its meaning not only its contemporary meaning but also the weight of over 1500 years of church tradition. Although 'language about the three persons of the Trinity is ultimately silence before mystery' this 'does not mean nothing is to be said before we reach the doors of the sanctuary behind which silence prevails.' *ibid* 600–601.

38 See HA Wolfson, *The Philosophy of the Church Fathers. Faith, Trinity, Incarnation*. 3rd ed. Rev., Mass Harvard University Press, 1976. The Apologists, as philosophers, faced a twofold problem: firstly, how can immaterial being be counted as three, if, according to Aristotle, anything which is numerical must be material? Secondly, how can the three be one? Their solution was to argue contrary to Philo and argue not for an absolute unity, but a relative unity: 'a unity which would allow within it a combination of three distinct elements.' 307–317.

39 K Surin, *The Turnings of Darkness and Light. Essays in Philosophical and Systematic Theology*, Cambridge: CUP, 1989, 30–31.

40 Martland, *op cit* 252–253.

41 GL Prestige, *God in Patristic Thought*. London: SPCK, 1985 vol.6, 225.

42 B Otis, 'Cappadocian Thought as a Coherent System', *Dumbarton Oaks Papers*, 12, Mass: Harvard University Press, 1958, 95–124, 107.

43 See ER Hardy, *Christology of the Later Fathers*, Philadelphia: The Westminster Press, 1954, 241–244.

44 Basil of Caeserea, *Letters*, NPNF[2] vol.VIII, Michigan: Wm.B.Eerdmans Publishing Company, 1978, CCXIV.4, 254.

45 Gregory of Nazianzus, *The Theological Orations*, NPNF[2] vol.VII, Michigan: Wm.B.Eerdmans Publishing Company, 1978, 3, XVI, 306.

46 Kelly *op cit* 262. Basil underlines this in his use of two different movements: knowledge of God is from the Spirit, through the Son to the Father. Goodness and holiness extend from the Father, through the Son to the Holy Spirit. *De Spirito Sancto*, XVIII.47, NPNF[2] vol.VII, 29. See B Bobrinskoy, 'The Indwelling of the Spirit in Christ.

"Pneumatic Christology" in the Cappadocian Fathers.' *St Vladimir's Theological Quarterly*, vol.28.1, 1984, 49–65, **55-58**.

[47] Gregory of Nyssa, *On Not Three Gods*, Christology of the Later Fathers, vol.III, Philadelphia: Westminster Press, MCMLIV, 261.

[48] HB Swete, *The Holy Spirit in the Ancient Church*, MacMillan and Co. Ltd., 165.

[49] *Letters, op cit*, CLXXXIX.7–8, 231.

[50] *Contra Macedonians*.

[51] *Theological Orations*, 5.X

[52] *ibid* 5.XXVI.

[53] In the Third Constantinople Lecture, RPC Hanson states, 'We may . . . accept the Nicene Creed as the end of the process of the formation of the church's doctrine of the Trinity.' *The Making of the Doctrine of the Trinity*, Anglican and Eastern Churches Association, 1984, 1. EL Mascall, however, states the situation more clearly, whilst commenting on 2 Cor.13:14, 'I would hold that there is a line of homogeneous development from the implicit but definite trinitarianism of the text of St. Paul to the explicit and systematic teaching of documents such as the so-called Athanasian Creed . . . What I want to stress is that the discussion is still a living one.' *The Triune God. An Ecumenical Study*, Worthing: Churchman Publishing Ltd, 1986, 7. Although Hanson may be correct in suggesting that trinitarian formulations undoubtedly have been moulded by Nicea, Mascall is nearer the truth in stating that the debate continues today.

[54] CW4, 235.

[55] CW4, 236.

[56] CW4, 509.

[57] CW4, 246. There is much that we could infer here, at the very least that he seems to suggest a *beginning* to the Son. However, within the full context of his theology this is certainly not the case. Whilst the verb implies a beginning Irving's use of it here is consistent with traditional usage.

[58] K Barth, *The Knowledge of God and the service of God according to the teaching of the Reformation*, London: Hodder and Stoughton Publishers, 1949, 25.

[59] CW4, 264.

[60] See GD Kaufman, *An Essay in Theological Method*, Missoula: Scholars Press, 1979, 37–39 for further example.

[61] JP Mackey, *The Christian Experience of God as Trinity*, London: SCM Press Ltd, 1983, 173.

[62] See B Bobrinskoy, *op cit* for a more recent development of Cappadocian pneumatology, as well as CM LaCugna, *God For Us*, San Fransisco: Harper Collins, 1992.

[63] See E Jüngel, *The Doctrine of The Trinity*, Edinburgh: Scottish Academic Press, 1976.

[64] CW4, 232.

[65] Augustine: *The Trinity*, trans. S McKenna, Washington DC: The Catholic University of America Press, 1981[3], 15, 17, 29.

[66] Richard of St. Victor: *Book Three of the Trinity*, trans. GA Zinn, London: SPCK, 1979. *Benjamin Minor*, trans. SV Yanowski. West Germany: Wiedfeld & Mehl, 1960.

[67] CW4, 263.

[68] *ibid*.

[69] See CE Gunton, 'The Spirit as the Transcendent Lord', in *Different Gospels*, ed. A Walker, London: SPCK, 1993.

[70] CW4, 265.

[71] PW1, 335.

[72] CW1, 263–264, italics mine.

[73] CW1, 263–264.

[74] Barth, CD, 1.1, 479.

[75] M Maus, 'A Category of the Human Mind' in *Category of the Person*, eds. M Carrithers, S Collins, S Lukes, Cambridge: CUP, 1986, 18ff.

[76] MV Anastos, 'Basil's Κατὰ Ευνομίου, A Critical Analysis' in *Basil of Caeserea: Christian Humanist, Ascetic. Part One*, ed. PJ Fedwick, Toronto: Pontifical Institute of Mediaeval Studies, 1981, 67–136, 129.

[77] Basil, *Letters, op cit* CXXV.375.

[78] *ibid* CCIII, CXIV.

[79] *Orations, op cit*, 43, 68–69.

[80] A Meredith, 'The Pneumatology of the Cappadocian Fathers and the Creed of Constantinople,' *Irish Theological Quarterly*, vol.48, 1981, 196–211, 4.

[81] JD Zizioulas, *Credo in Spiritum Sanctum*, Atti del congresso teologi-cal internationale di Pneumatologia, Rome: Vaticana Libreria Editrice, 32.

[82] JD Zizioulas, *Being as Communion*, London: Darton, Longman and Todd Ltd, 1985, 42.

[83] *ibid*, 44. Schleiermacher makes a very perceptive and critical comment regarding such an interpretation which directly addresses the theological method assumed by Zizioulas, but one of which Irving is not guilty.

'They identify the Father with the unity of the Divine Essence, but not the Son or the Spirit. This can be traced right back to the idea of Origen, that the Father is God absolutely, while Son and Spirit are God only by participation in the Divine essence—an idea which is positively rejected by orthodox Church teachers, but secretly under-lies their whole procedure.' *The Christian Faith*, §171.5, 747.

[84] Letter 38.4, NPNF[2] vol.VIII, 139.

[85] *ibid*.

[86] Gregory of Nyssa, *On Not Three Gods op cit*, 266.

[87] See Richard of St. Victor, *supra*.

[88] E Jüngel, *op cit*, 30.

[89] M Polanyi, *Personal Knowledge. Towards a Post-Critical Philosophy*, London: Routledge & Kegan Paul, 1987, ch.5, 69–131.

[90] Schœnberg, *Moses und Aron*, Uxbridge: The Hillingdon Press, 1974, Act 1, Scenes 1, 2, 4.

[91] *ibid*, Act 1 Scene 2.

92 *ibid*, Act 2 Scene 4.
93 John 1:8.
94 CW5, 408–409.
95 CW5, 87.
96 CW5, 87–88.
97 CW5, 170.
98 CW4, 231.
99 CW4, 229.
100 CW4, 231.
101 *ibid*.
102 CW4, 240.
103 CW4, 231. Although Irving draws from both Augustine and the more recent influence of Hooker, he deviates from both in this understanding of theophany. Both the former argue that the entire Godhead appeared to the Fathers, and that the entire Divine nature became incarnate in Christ. See Augustine, *De Trinitate*, 2:8,9,12. R Hooker, *The Works of Mr Richard Hooker. In Eight Books of the Laws of Ecclesiastical Polity*, London: William Baynes & Sons, 1822, V. 51:2.
104 CW4, 337.
105 CW4, 343.
106 CW4, 338.
107 CW4, 270. (see *ibid* 270–271 where Irving expounds his trinal method in detail. See also CW5, 414).
108 *ibid*.
109 CW4, 271.
110 *ibid*. This entire argument is expounded in detail in CW5, 350–361.
111 CW5, 408.
112 CW5, 406.
113 CW4, 404.
114 CW5, 405.
115 CW5, 406.
116 For further details on this qualification, see, D Wendebourg, 'From the Cappadocian Fathers to Gregory Palamas. The Defeat of Trinitarian Theology,' *Studia Patristica* ed. EA Livingstone, Vol.XVII: Part 1, 194–1948, Oxford: Pergamon Press, 1982.
117 DW Hardy, 'Coleridge On The Trinity' *The Anglican Theological Review*, LXIX:2, 1988, 145–155.
118 CW5, 12.
119 CW5, 13.
120 CW5, 347.
121 CW5, 406.
122 CW5, 408.
123 CW5, 409.
124 The manner in which Irving identifies divine activity is similar to that suggested by the dynamic reciprocal penetration implicit in the Greek notion of *perichoresis*. It is of interest to note that his method does not favour the more traditional Western approach of *circuminessio* which implies the idea of a more static coinherence in repose. In this sense,

Irving stands much more close to the Cappadocian stress on the diversity of persons, rather that the Western notion of unity. (See W Kasper, *The God of Jesus Christ*, London: SCM Press Ltd., 1984, 284).

[125] JR Barth, *Coleridge and Christian Tradition*, Cambridge: Harvard University Press, 1969, 104. This will be expanded in more detail in Part III.

[126] ST Coleridge, *Specimens of the Table Talk of Samuel Taylor Coleridge*, 4th edition, May 15, 1830, London: John Murray, 1851, 73.

[127] MSB³ f.277. Cited in JR Barth, *op cit*, 91.

[128] Notebook 36, f.51. Cited in JM Boulger, *Coleridge as Religious Thinker*, New Haven: Yale University Press, 1961, 141.

# Part II

# Irving's Doctrine of Human Being

## Introduction

> Why talk of a heavenly flesh, when you have no grounds to offer
> us for your celestial theory? Why deny it to be earthy, when you
> have the best reasons for knowing it to be earthy? He hungered
> under the devil's *temptations*; He thirsted with the woman of
> Samaria; He wept over Lazarus; He trembles at death (for 'the
> flesh,' as He says 'is weak'); At last He pours out blood. These,
> I suppose, are celestial marks?[1]

However much the Christian belief of an incarnated God is
expounded, there will always be the lurking threat of
Docetism, the subtle question that undermines any appreciation that God in Christ took to himself a truly physical
existence. Such is the legacy of the Graeco-Roman context
within which Christianity took root, a context within which
matter and spirit were perceived to be opposites. In such a
context it is, indeed, difficult to state how the divine and, by
nature, pure Spirit, can both assume the human and, by
nature, material existence, as well as endure our common
infirmities. Small wonder, then, that Docetic christologies
have contaminated our notion of incarnation. The notion of
two distinct worlds, the noumenal and the material, which
have permeated thought from Parmenides through Plato to
Kant and up to present materialist ideologies, has influenced
the very assumptions we bring to the doctrine of the
incarnation. Such assumptions are expressed in the ancient
flight from the material through to their modern reverse,
the flight from the spiritual. In dialogue with as well as in

69

bondage to both forms of thought, the Christian faith has sought to assert the belief that both worlds have met in the person and history of Jesus Christ. 'That which was from the beginning, which we have heard, which we have seen with our eyes, which we have looked upon and touched with our hands . . . we proclaim to you.'[2] In fact, 'very' God takes on 'very' man.

This basic Christian belief has assumed multiform expression, in which, for the most part, Tertullian's comment above fits unsquarely. His comment, perhaps, represents the very boundaries of language when we talk about the sort of humanity assumed in incarnation. Yet, at the same time, it would be true to say that the sentiments expressed by Tertullian waned under the cut and thrust of more relevant and pressing issues in the debate about the meeting of the divine and human in Jesus Christ. So much so that the assertion that the divine and human, the creator and created, the infinite and the finite have come together in the event of incarnation, has strangely mutated into its very opposite. The divine has been partitioned to the realm of the unknown; we can only interact with the visible, tangible and audible. Consequently, our pictures of Christ are blurred under the apparently insurmountable modern problem of addressing Jesus Christ as a revelation of the divine. A complete break appears to have occurred with the past.[3]

This Copernican shift highlights the debate in which Irving found himself. Yet there was very much a sense of having to avoid two clear dangers. On the one hand, he addressed a theological climate on the verge of modernity, with its temptation to present an ever increasingly human interpretation of Jesus Christ. The anthropocentric was rapidly replacing the theocentric. On the other hand, there was the aristocratic presence of Docetism where the humanity of Jesus was given only token significance. What is of interest concerning Irving is that he offers a response to both dangers. He is clearly reacting against the latter. Yet he does so within the context of the former. There is, perhaps, room for suggestion that Irving finds space to articulate his own particular christology because already the climate is more open to human presentations of Christ, remembering that it

is not without significance that his most immediate theological counterpart is Schleiermacher, who himself sought to
develop a more realistic presentation of Jesus Christ.

Therefore, to an extent, Irving can be interpreted as being
in touch with this development which itself was a healthy
reaction against too transcendent an interpretation of the
Christ-event. Yet his solution does not entail a flight from
the divine. Rather, he reappraises the relationship between
the divine and the human within the context of incarnation.
It was suggested in the previous chapter that had Irving's
opponents better understood his doctrine of God, they
would have more clearly grasped his own doctrine of the
incarnation. Yet, at the same time his doctrine of God was
so out of step with the time that, had they understood it,
they would probably have had more fuel to add to the fire!
Similarly, had they understood his doctrine of human being
they would have understood his stress on the type of human
nature assumed in incarnation and seen it as an attempt to
address some of the problems he faced as he preached the
gospel. However, in so doing, they would have been
confronted by a doctrine of human being as distinctive as his
doctrine of God.

For Irving, the reappraisal of what he had inherited
demanded, to some extent, a shift in understanding concerning the Spirit's role in incarnation. This, in turn, entailed an
understanding of the Spirit in relation both to the triune God
and to the incarnate Son. In the previous chapter we have
seen how Irving outlines this within a trinitarian principle of
revelation: the incarnate Son reveals the nature and character of the triune God. In and through Christ we see God as
Father, Son and Spirit. The dynamic of revelation, however,
does not stop with the divine: in addition to it, we are also
privy to the true nature of the human. For Irving, the two
are deeply rooted in the historical Christ: the other-worldly
existence of the divine is rooted in the very stuff of human
existence. In so doing, Irving stands firmly in line with the
opening comments of Calvin's *Institutes*:

Without knowledge of self there is no knowledge of God.
Nearly all the wisdom we possess, that is to say, sure and sound

wisdom, consists of two parts: the knowledge of God and of ourselves.[4]

However, whereas Calvin did not need to clarify the relationship between the human and the divine to the degree Irving felt necessary for his own time, Irving can be interpreted as extending Calvin's maxim by making more explicit the role of Christ. He does so in a manner that represents an anticipation of Barth's comment on Calvin above, that, 'we cannot accept the theses of Calvin unless we transplant them from the empty and rather speculative sphere in which they stand in his thinking, and root them once more in the firm ground of the knowledge of Jesus Christ in which they really grew even in Calvin'.[5]

For Calvin, Irving and Barth, the incarnation prevents any attempt to describe God's relation to the world in terms of logical complements. Rather, the revelation by Jesus Christ of both the divine and the human must be understood in a way that integrates them. The question, however, is just how we do this. For Irving it means unpacking his doctrine of human being against the backdrop of his doctrine of God as revealed in and through Jesus Christ. And in particular, for Irving, at the heart of the matter is the problem of being and how it is perceived. If divine and human being are understood as logical opposites, then the problem remains insurmountable. The modern reaction to some traditional incarnational theology is justified in both form and content. Yet, for Irving, any presentation of divine and human being as logical opposites results in a very impaired understanding of being *per se*. This, in turn, has direct implications concerning the kind of salvation offered through faith in Christ.

In what way, then, does Irving attempt to bridge this impasse? In Part I we saw how he highlights the missing role of the Spirit. Without a proper understanding of the Spirit's personal identity, we have an impaired perception of the very grounds of being itself. If this is so we should be hardly surprised to discover that the Achilles' heel in our understanding of Christ is to be found in this pneumatological area. That is, our perception, or rather, lack of perception of the Spirit's role in incarnation, has led to an emaciated appreciation of the true humanity of Christ. It is only a small step, then, to rather inadequate Christian interpretations of human being in general.

Irving, as we have seen in our previous chapter, seeks to address this problem in his doctrine of God which facilitates a more consistently trinitarian understanding of the God who relates as Father, Son and Spirit. In turn, he applies this to his understanding of the person and humanity of Christ. The purpose of this chapter is to outline the way in which Irving relates the human with the divine in such a way as to make sense of the role of the Spirit in incarnation.

In order to do this, we must turn our attention to Irving's doctrine of human being, the most neglected area of his entire theology. To this date, there has been no direct examination of Irving's supposedly unorthodox christology with direct reference to his anthropology.[6] That this is the case is a somewhat ironic statement upon institutional, theological procedure. It was on the very basis of his understanding of human being that Irving faced the full vehemence of his mother church. Yet it was by means of such concepts that Irving sought to present a christology which both addressed and grappled with the traditional questions concerning sin and salvation which can be summarized in Kelsey's words:

1. What is it about human being that makes it possible for them in their finitude to know the infinite God?
2. What is it about human being that makes fallenness possible in such a radical way as to require the kind of redemption to which Christianity witnesses?[7]

It is to this neglected element of Irving's thought and his answer to such questions that our attention now turns; as the hermeneutical key that unlocks his entire thought and for an understanding of how his doctrine of human being is of fundamental importance to unlocking his christology.

## Strange News from Another Star[8]

The rabbinic tradition of Israel recounts a tale about the creation of the world. Having completed creating everything in five days, the Creator asked one of the attending angels whether anything were still missing. The angel answered that everything was, of course, perfect, as one might expect of God's own handiwork. 'Yet perhaps,' the angel ventured, 'perhaps one thing could make this already perfect work more perfect: speech, to praise its perfection.' God thereupon approved the angel's words and created the human creature.[9]

The speaking God, *Deus loquens*, provides his own text and narrative. He creates by his own speech. Behold! the speaking creature. And it is by means of this speaking creature that the Creator provides a new language: his Word itself is enfleshed. In the very act of incarnation the speaking God learns the language of humanity and does so with a very specific intention that this creature should again learn to echo the primordial, divine narrative. Perhaps it is in this sense that we should interpret Calvin's sentiments above.[10] Knowledge of the human can be understood to facilitate true knowledge of the divine.

In terms of how we know God, then, this suggests that the anthropological dimension to any statement about Christ is of major importance. This involves an understanding of our human origins. Christian cosmogonies and cosmologies, that is, theories about the origin of the universe and treatises on the structure of creation, respectively, have by and large explained our origins in terms of conflict between either archaeological or teleological interpretations of creation, that is, by focusing on either our origins or an anticipated goal. On the whole, the dominant interpretation has been the former: we understand ourselves in relation to where we *began*. The fall from an originally perfect state necessitates a return to that original state of perfection in which the first human beings were created. Human being is explained in terms of its beginning. Unfortunately, this tends towards a rather static interpretation of human being: a qualitative commodity that, having lost is original perfection, seeks to find it again in a prototype. However, in the light of our increasing knowledge of the human condition such a return to paradise lost comes, as 'strange news from another star'.

The teleological approach, on the other hand, seeks to

understand human being in terms of where is it is *going* and, in particular, where it will end. It entails a more developmental and progressive interpretation of human history. We are freed from the determinism of our past. We are more able to be understood in dynamic and relational terms. It is from this direction that Irving reads the human narrative —our beginning is determined by the conclusion. Thus he asserts,

> I believe God hath ordained nature in its present form, and established it according to its present laws, for the single and express purpose of shadowing forth that future perfect condition into which it is to be brought so that from man down to the lowest creation. . . . everything containeth the presentiment of its own future perfection.[11]

This alone, however, is insufficient for Irving. He subordinates this teleological interpretation of the human story to a more primary narrative which serves to prevent any diminution of the human predicament. So he writes,

> We must receive our first principles of cosmogony from revelation, and adopt them as the card by which we steer our course of action, before ever our intercourse with the visible world, or human life, will leave behind it any soil upon which the seed of the word will take root and flourish.[12]

Irving's cosmogony is derived, then, from his prior understanding of God: *all* things are created in and through Christ, and, as we shall see in Part III, this he interprets as a creation in and through the eternal Son. In the very act of creating, the Son acts not in the blazing glory of infinite Godhead, but, as it were, through the reduced and fracted beam of created being, his future assumed form of being. Consequently, Irving's doctrine of creation is safeguarded from the threat of anthropocentrism, that is, of putting human being at the centre, since creation has its being and meaning only in and through the Son of God.

As such, human history has personal meaning: it takes its entire rationale from Christ, start to finish. What is of importance here is the fact that, for Irving, we do not attribute the Son's significance only to his saving, but also to his creating work. To this extent, Irving presents us with a theology in which the Creator and the Saviour are inextricably united in the act of creation, not merely salvation. Creation has an appointed end because it is is one with the humanity of the Son, its Creator then Redeemer. It finds its meaning in and through the history of the incarnated Son. For this reason, the end and meaning of human history is destroyed within that of the Son.

## Master-Story 1: Paradise Gained

> Men look on the starry heavens with reverence: monkeys do not . . . When we are frightened by the greatness of the universe, we are (almost literally) frightened by our own shadows for these light years and billions of centuries are mere arithmetic until the shadow of man, the poet, the maker of myth, falls upon them. I do not say we are wrong to tremble at his shadow; it is a shadow of an image of God. But if ever the vastness of matter threatens to overcross our spirits, one must remember that it is matter spiritualized which does so. To puny man, the great nebula in Andromeda owes in a sense its greatness.[13]

According to biblical creation stories, the arrival of human being onto the platform of history announces the highest form of being in the created world. It is the culmination of the Creator God's activity, after which is sabbath. For Irving, however, the creation of human being is to be considered neither as complete nor as an end in itself. Rather, it finds its ultimate meaning in the Creator's purpose for creation. This purpose Irving considers from several perspectives.

Firstly, from a theological perspective, the creature is created in order that God may 'find the justification of his holiness, and the upholding of it forever'.[14] The creature exists 'to bring the invisible mind of God to light' in order that God 'may be seen and known in his working over creation'.[15] Human being, therefore, is created with the express purpose of revealing 'unto all the creatures the invisible and infinite substance of the Godhead',[16] to 'body forth God completely in all the features and powers of his invisible Godhead'.[17]

Secondly, creation has a christological function: the great end of creation consists for the 'manifestation of the Son of God in the creature form of the risen God-man, in which to abide and act is the will of God the Father for ever',[18] thus enabling the creature 'to represent, to enact, and to enjoy a part of his fulness (Col.1: 15–20)'.[19]

Thirdly, there is an anthropic dimension: by virtue of the Creator's act of creation from nothing, human being is dependent being. It is so by virtue of the humble origins of its existence, for 'as He was to make it out of nothing, He would have it remember its nothingness in itself . . . to this single end of bringing the creature to apprehend the nothingness of its substance, and the absoluteness of its dependence upon the divine Will, which is the very truth'.[20]

Each will be considered throughout this chapter. However, Irving gathers all these different but interrelated considerations under the ultimate purpose of God in creating human being, which he understands in the following manner:

> The purpose of God in creating man, was the manifestation and communication of His own glory unto the creatures which He had made, or which He was about to make; and to bring the creature wholly dependent upon Him, and to worship Him.[21]

Consequently, the purpose and end of creation finds its ultimate meaning not in human being itself, but in its dependency upon God who brings it into existence in the first place. It is being-in-relation: the creature dependent upon the Creator who is the very source of its existence and being.

We have, at this point, set the scene against which we may begin to give Irving's answer to the initial questions set out by Kelsey at the beginning of this chapter: human being is created with the express purpose of revealing the glory of God. Essential to this purpose is the notion that human

being is being-in-relation. The question to ask, then,
concerns the dynamics of this relatedness.

Irving's answer turns on two symbols derived from the
creation story in Genesis 1:27–28 wherein 'God created man
in his own image, in the image of God he created him; male
and female he created them. And God blessed them and
God said to them, "Be fruitful and multiply, and fill the
earth and subdue it; and have dominion over the fish of the
sea and over the birds of the air and over every living thing
that moves upon the earth." ' The divine mandate to be
both image bearer and lord of creation becomes the 'charter
and the law, the frame' of human being. Both expressions
declare something about the divine purpose behind the
creation of human beings, namely, that God may have 'His
own invisible and incomprehensible essence, and to give to
this likeness of Himself the primacy and lordship of all
creation.' It is of fundamental importance to Irving's doctrine of human being that whatever form the creature takes,
it cannot thwart an anterior principle to that of creation, that
is, the will of the Creator that the 'fiat of God for human
kind is that which still abideth unalterable'.[22]

Irving's entire theology may be understood as a commentary on his understanding of the term 'image of God'. It
serves, as it were, as a 'tensive symbol', that is, as 'an idea or
doctrine which collects (and thus to some extent simplifies)
and represents a range of meanings and issues'.[23] For Irving,
this symbol contained together several important issues.
Firstly, it represented the very charter of human being,
which consists in the command to be 'Godlike, an image and
likeness of God in the law and form of (its) being'.[24] In Part
I we saw how Irving establishes the identity of the Son as the
image of the Father. This, in turn, becomes the means by
which he understands human being: it is the *imago Dei*, the
image of God. When the Creator-God, the Father, pro-
claims and brings about the high end of creation in creating
man and woman, he does so as God the Father who bears
witness to the Son. There is, then, no hint of abstraction in
Irving's doctrine of human being. The identity of the human
creature is a very particular one: it is as an image of God
after the likeness of the Son.

> Within Himself from all eternity there was an image of Himself
> in the person of the Eternal Son: out of Himself that image is
> found in man; first in the person of Christ, and then in every one
> who is renewed after the image of God in righteousness and true
> holiness.[25]

From this we are able to address two aspects of his thought.
Firstly, Irving maintains a very clear tension in his interpretation of the *imago Dei*. Christ is both the beginning and the
end of human being: that which is imaged and that which
perfectly images. As such, by imaging the Son who is the
express image of the Father, human being can be understood as deriving its entire being from its relation to God the
Son. Let us look at this in particular in relation to the origins
of human existence.

What does it mean to talk of a christocentric interpretation of the image of God? For Irving it means that human
being is derived from the very one it mirrors. To this extent,
Irving stands in the mainstream of Reformation thought.
Human being reflects the image of the Son and does so by
'conformity of an intelligent will to the will and Word of
God'.[26] Both aspects are united in our second point of
clarification, the notion of being-in-relation.

Part I highlighted how Irving understands the Son to be
the image of the invisible Father. In this sense, the concept
of 'image' essentially entails the notion of reflection: the Son
is the reflection of the Father who at all times remains
unrevealed. This notion of imaging, in turn, is inextricably
linked to the idea of obedience on the part of the Son and
obedience Irving understands in terms of the Son's dependence upon the Spirit. We can understand this, then, as a
reflection-in-dependence. If we apply this notion of reflection to human existence, we may extend to the human
creature as the image of God, the same notion of reflection.
As such, human being lacks an essential ability to fulfil itself.
As the Son fulfils his own potential as one called to reflect
the Father through the Spirit, so too with the human
creature we attain our potential as images of God only to the
degree we, too, fulfil our own calling as we depend on the
Spirit.[27] Irving, then, anticipates Torrance's comment on

Calvin, that 'the *imago Dei*, spiritually considered, has no momentum or security of its own, but depends entirely upon the grace of God and is maintained only in relation to that grace'.[28] For Irving, this grace is to be understood not merely in terms of salvation, but can be traced back to the very act of creation itself.

## *Imago Dei: the divine part among the earthly*

What is it that makes possible a link between the Saviour and the creature? Irving finds the point of contact in the idea of human being as being-in-reflection, as the image of God. Throughout his writings, from the earliest sermons to the later apologetical publications, he is consistent in his belief that human being is created as the image of God in order 'to act the divine part among earthly scenes'.[29] How, then, does Irving explain this order in creation? To answer this question we must turn our attention to how he understands male and female as the bearers of the image of God.

'Man,' he summarises most concisely in the *Morning Watch*, 'was created for two ends: the first, "to be an image and likeness of God"; the second, "to have dominion over the creatures".' It is the former that concerns us here, for it is, 'descriptive of his reasonable soul . . . fashioned on very purpose to be an image of God, who is Spirit; endowed with his affections of love and goodness, of truth and justice, of wisdom and understanding: . . . so that God without any accommodations should be able to speak his mind to man, and man without any conjecture should be able to understand it'.[30]

We may pause at this point to question how consistent Irving is in his description of the image. Hitherto, it has been interpreted solely in terms of the Son. This is not the whole story, however: human being consists also of spirit.

> In virtue of this conformity of human reason to the infinite Spirit of God, in virtue of man's soul being an image and likeness of God, God was able to converse with Adam in the garden of Eden, as afterwards he did with Abraham and Moses, and doth with us all in his word. For the word of God is not an

accommodation but a real utterance of God's mind to man's mind, created for the very purpose of understanding and responding to God.[31]

In the conformity of human reason to infinite Spirit the true identity of God is revealed. The image, therefore, does not consist merely of a moral propensity to good, nor even in the mutuality of human sexual differentiation, as with Barth.[32] Rather, Irving locates the capacity for image-bearing in the human will. It is this notion of the will that becomes the leitmotif, the controlling concern, for Irving's doctrine of human being.

Intimately linked to the notion of human will as the means by which the divine and the human meet, is the notion of freedom. Human being is the image of one who is unrestrained.[33] It is because 'God is free and uncaused, being the cause of himself' that 'man must have, and hath, such a part in his will, which within the creature-bound is caused by nothing, but is of itself the cause'.[34] Thus Irving maintains the notion of human being as image bearer of the Creator God in terms of the creature's will and its original freedom. The very constitution of human being resides in the will, whereby the human creature 'is a figure of God; the will answering to the Father, in that it is a cause unto itself, not caused by things without or motives within, but free in its proper constitution to originate all thought and action'.[35]

God's freedom from being subject to causality is seen in his ability both to be what he wills himself to be and to remain so. Such freedom from determinism also constitutes the very nature of human existence. As God is perfectly free from any form of causation, so 'it required that there should be in man, his image, a will which should be uncaused, the cause of itself; not overmastered by God, but left to act in its own liberty'.[36] Freedom of will in the human creature reflects the very character of God, who is himself perfectly free and uncaused.

Why does Irving stress this element of freedom, of being uncaused? Firstly, as noted above, human beings are constituted according to the Creator's design: the human creature should be like God, and be so by its own will.[37] Secondly we are created to relate to God and willingly serve him freely. Lastly, it is by means of our own free will that we are able, in turn, to relate to the world around.

We can see, then, that for Irving, there is a very strong connection between creation in general and the notion of the will, both human and divine, in particular. But what exactly does Irving mean by this? In order to clarify his position we can approach it from two different but complementary perspectives. Firstly, there is the relation of the divine to the human. It is created with the 'very purpose to bring the invisible mind of God to light, to be his likeness, through which he may be seen and known in his working over the creation'.[38] The former, as image bearer, is derived from the latter: it is a being-in-relation. Consequently, it operates in conjunction with the one with whom it has a relationship, namely God. Irving understands the dynamic of the relationship as such:

> Now God, being a Spirit, carrieth on his communication only through the Spirit or word, and not other wise. There his operation as God beginneth and endeth. He leaves the will of the man to do the rest.[39]

It is because God is 'spirit and not flesh, invisible and not visible, insensible and not sensible, operating as God doth operate, by power of a word, not by physical contact'[40] that the divine action with the human is an operation in the human spirit, which Irving identifies as the will. At this point, we have arrived at the centre of Irving's entire doctrine of human being. Human being is contingent being, that is, it is dependent upon God who, as pure Spirit, relates to the human by means of its spirit, namely, its will.

At first glance, Irving appears to be advocating yet another split-perspective: the material and spiritual appear to be pitted against one another. On closer inspection, however, this is no dualism. He affirms the New Testament's proclamation of two states of being, the old and new Adams, as argued by Paul in his epistle to the Christians at Rome. For Irving, as Paul, Adam is representative of two very distinct responses to the divine initiatives of creation and redemption. The second Adam is not so much spiritual as he is material: in his obedience to God he actualizes his true nature, over against the first Adam who, by his act of disobedience, negates his true humanity. There is no dualism since Irving is very much at pain to stress the goodness of the material in its relation to the spiritual. Irving's is a high anthropology: the material is *good*. Any repudiation of the materiality of human existence is to affirm something that is less than human and an offence against the high dignity he perceived to lie at the very heart of human existence. This attitude comes to good effect in a sermon in which he denounces those who oppose the idea of eating in the afterlife. He responds by asserting,

> I know what a body-despising Puritan (falsely called spiritual) generation I am speaking to; men who, not understanding the question of materialism at all, nor seeing the glory of God in it, have an ignorant prejudice against the whole subject, and a pitiful fear of it, as holding of the materialist school. Poor wits! what are you afraid of? Has not God made me with a body? and is He not to raise me again with a body? and is there not to be a new earth as well as a new heaven? What makes you so much outcry about, ye disciples of the shadowy elysium of the heathens? I would you had more reverence for God's material creation, and for man's body, creation's lord.[41]

The question to be answered now concerns the manner in which Irving holds together the material and spiritual aspects of human existence. To answer this we turn to his understanding of the original human state.

## Human Being: the vinculum creationis

The ultimate primacy of human being over the created order, according to Irving, is to be found in its unique status. It is both *imago mundi* and *imago Dei*, that is, an image of both the created and the Creator. As image of God, human being is being-with. It exists with the capacity to transcend itself, step beyond its own boundaries, and relate firstly to God and then to others of its kind. However, as one who images the world, the created order, it is being-in. It has an 'earthed' existence. Whilst he is the one with raised arm and upward gaze, he is so as one with feet and legs rooted firmly in the created world. Thus, human being is *imago mundi* by virtue of being-in, for it shares its existence with the immanent and non-personal world around it.

Human being, then, is both being-in and being-with: it is both immanent and transcendent. As such it is the *vinculum creationis*, that which links both spirit and matter within creation.

For Irving, this is the original design for human being: it was at first 'a body of dust, and a spirit from God; by the one holding of the creature, by the other of the Creator; and so in himself forming a link between the creature and the Creator'.[42] The great link between the two is the capacity of the human will to make responses to its Creator, albeit a capacity based on divine grace, for, 'he would have the will of man to be recognised as the lord of all visible things'.[43] Thus, for Irving spiritual life is 'the life of the spirit . . . the constant presence of a will to live so'.[44] In so doing, he presents not only our spirituality in terms of obedient will, but human 'perfection in terms of one whose will, word and work is in unison with God's'.[45]

Yet, whilst the human will is the meeting place between the Creator and the created, the divine and the human, it is the purely material aspect of human existence that is, for Irving, the *conditio sine qua non* by which this occurs due to the fact that 'the body is the organ by which the spirit within a man doth manifest itself to the world'.[46] It is, consequently, as an embodied creature that the figure of Adam surpasses angelic existence and is able to bear the divine image. For, as Irving points out, incorporeal beings such as angels have no need of a material body in order to be fulfilled: they are pure spirit, perfect in their kind. But not so with Adam, who as the link between the spiritual and the physical introduces not only an altogether new form of existence, but one that is superior to all other forms of created existence.

The creation of Adam hath this advancement, above the creation of angels, that it includeth another kind of existence, any one substance, and any one exponent of the Divine Mind and purpose, which is the visible, as distinguished from the invisible; the corporeal, as distinguished from the incorporeal; matter, as distinguished from spirit. Hitherto there had only been invisible and incorporeal substance, which is as the the soul of man; but now there is to be joined therewith a body which shall possess all material and visible things as its habitation.[47]

When Irving turns his attention to the more material aspect of human existence he uses the notion of dominion to establish the high dignity of human being within the world of creation. On the one hand, as the image of God, the human is a being-under-dominion. It owes and finds its existence in God. Yet, on the other hand, the creature mirrors its image: it is a being-in-dominion. Irving uses the latter in order to outline the place of the human within creation. At all times, however, this being-in-relation is itself part of a wider context of relationships. Thus Irving asserts,

God, when He had finished His work, gave it into the charge and responsibility of man it was man's house, for man's government; always in obedience and subservience to God —which is a condition, the absolute condition, of a creature.[48]

Irving moves from the purely transcendent to both the purely material and the link between the two, human being. In so doing, he begins to outline a metaphysic which enables him to embrace and express the full scope of human existence, whose being-in-relation has three distinct foci: God, self and the extra-human.[49] These foci, however, are not to be divided between the terms, 'image of God' and 'dominion'. They are very much inter-related in Irving's anthropology, albeit in a very definite manner. The creature is created,

first and noblest of all, to be His own image and like-ness; but next, and only second to this, to be the heir, possessor, and lord of all His created works, to have dominion, to rule for God, to possess and to enjoy the works of His hands: this is an integrant part of man's creation;—to inherit the earth, the habitable earth; to have dominion over the beasts of the earth, the fish of the sea, and the fowls of the heaven; this, I say, upon God's own constituting Word, is as much of man's essential being as it is to be holy as God is holy, and pure as He is pure; and who is the man that dare gainsay it?[50]

The idea of dominion, significantly, is not a merely functional attribute of human being: it is essential to being human. In Adam, the archetype, human being 'stood as the head of the creation, sun, moon, and stars, and earth; the world animate and inanimate; creation's lord, who sealed up the sum full of wisdom and perfect in beauty, whom God also pronounced good'.[51] The created order is not given over as a mere habitation nor as a diversion for Adam and Eve. Rather, the appointment of the human creature to be creation's sovereign, carries with it immeasurable responsibility: human being has the capacity for changing creation, by means of its freedom to choose the good. Irving expands this in his understanding of dominion. He interprets it in purely human terms. The biblical notion of oneness of being and substance in male and female (Rom. 5: 12–21, 1 Cor. 15: 20–21) prepares the foundation for his use of Adam as a type. Consequently he writes:

These instances of the oneness of being and substance in a plurality of persons shew out the proper mystery of manhood, as distinct from the angelic nature; whose numbers were never thus recapitulated into one person as mankind were heretofore into Adam, and the saints are hereafter to be into Christ.[52]

However, what is of greater importance here is the use Irving makes of this creation mandate to outline the relationship between Adam and that over which he is appointed to be sovereign. As sovereign of creation he determines the destiny of that which he tends, or, as Irving puts it, the created order 'sinks or swims . . . falls or rises'[53] from its human sovereign. This denotes much more an essential than purely functional aspect to human identity. It is an affirmation of the first couple's relation to the created order: human being has an essential relation to that which the Creator calls 'good'. Consequently, to understand Irving here, we must recognize that the function of dominion belongs to the category of being: it is an ontological category which is prescriptive of human being. Thus, being-with-God is not a flight from matter. Rather, it is a resounding 'Yes', to the material. The truly human is humanity in the image of God as rooted and grounded in its physical environment.

This original intention of the Creator for his image bearer is revealed in a two-dimensional manner: in the human spirit to be God's likeness, and in the human body to 'express every disposition of God in the government of the creatures'. This notion of the relatedness between the human and the extra-human helps unpack, in turn, Irving's interpretation of the image of God in terms of responsibility: 'man is the responsible creature; he only is the responsible one: all the rest are subject to him, and look up to him; not to God directly, but to man directly, and through him their offering is to be presented to God'.[54] The one who is 'God-breathed' mirrors the divine only as one who is 'dust-formed'. The former may distinguish the image bearer from the impersonal world, but the latter defines the context within which this imaging occurs. It is a righteousness that manifests itself not only *in* the material, but also *by virtue* of it. Consequently, the material and spiritual dimensions of human existence are not polar opposites, but complementary elements of the one being. As such, Irving's doctrine of human being is a clear affirmation of the goodness of human existence, and is at all times the background out of which his explicit doctrine concerning the human nature of Christ is formed.[55]

Thus far Irving's anthropology has been outlined in terms of its relation both to the one it images, as *imago Dei*, and to that over which it has dominion, as *imago mundi*. We have investigated both the object imaged and the context within which this imaging occurs. What remains to be shown is the relation of the subject to itself within this context of relatedness. And so we turn to look at the way in which the image bearer is understood to be related to himself.

What is the inner dynamic by which this creature can be

the link between the created and the Creator? On the one
hand, Irving understands the human parallel with God in
terms of our reason, or spirit. As reasonable being, we are
open to the divine. Yet, as we have noted, the human spirit
is enfleshed spirit: it takes on a very real material and
physical existence. For Irving, the mind of God is imaged in
the soul, or reason, of man[56] and given a visible, finite and
material expression. For Irving, the human creature as
God's image and king is an 'embodied spirit'.[57] Irving
explains this apparent dualism in terms of a cultural analogy:

> The Jew and the Christian can be as little separated as the body
> and spirit of a living man; and, like these two constituents of a
> living man, neither can they be confused or mixed up with one
> another, but must be treated of as distinct, though co-essential
> to life.[58]

Irving draws from his doctrine of the Trinity to develop
further this tension between the material and spiritual.
Firstly, as noted above, he identifies the basic human
constitution as residing in the will. As God the Father is
supreme Will, so man is invested with the capacity to image
the divine since his was a will first created free from
causality. The Father's Will, in turn, is eternally expressed in
Reason, which Irving parallells with the Son. Lastly, this
Reason expresses itself in yet another form, the Spirit who
goes 'forth from the Father and the Word, in order to
express their will and their mind in outward action'.[59] And
when this is applied to the human creature as image of God,
Irving perceives it to be an imaging in terms of will, reason
and expression. Consequently, 'man in his constitution as a
creature, is a type of the constitution of the Creator, three
subsistencies on one substance, each complete and perfect in
itself, yet inseparable and indivisible from one another'.[60]
Perhaps here we detect the thoroughgoing understanding of
the Trinity that motivates Irving's entire theological endea-
vour. As God is Triune and thus internally self-relating so
human being is an inwardly self-relating being. For Irving,
like Coleridge, human being is understood as a dynamic
relation in the order of being.[61] However, Irving goes

beyond his Coleridgean influence: his stress on the saving significance of Christ freed him from any Coleridgean abstractions. In the same way that his context demanded a reinterpretation and reorientation of theology, so also did his anthropology take on a line that is Irving's alone. Like his contemporaries, Irving shared a concern in establishing a foundation for talking about the divine and human in the Christ-event. However, unlike Kant who presented Christ as an ideal against whom human beings are seen to fail, or Schleiermacher who represented Christ as the ideal and perfect expression of religious Christian consciousness, or Hegel whose christology is seen to transform human life whilst not necessarily being dependent upon the historical Jesus, Irving's aim is to present a christology that preserves a trinitarian dynamic and the very practical significance of the incarnation.[62] Divine reason and will correspond to human reason and will. His is a moral interpretation of creation, and one which attempts to describe the dynamics of human morality in such a way as to answer how the 'infinite can be focused in the finite . . . and the unconditioned ideal be instantiated in a historic individual'.[63] What is of interest, then, in Irving's response is that it attempts to answer such questions without falling into the anthropocentric interpretations of human being given by Kant and Schleiermacher.

Irving begins by defining the limits of human being: the flesh. Flesh delimits human existence. It is 'the bound and compass which God hath fixed for the definition of His creature man', not simply the body, nor merely the soul, but the body and soul, or spirit, in unison. It denotes both the visible and invisible existing in union with one another.[64] The 'soulish' element, whilst evidently non-material, exists only by virtue of the material. Flesh and blood delineate 'the region of the will and power of man.'[65] Human being is, therefore, enfleshed being, or embodied spirit. This non-material dimension to human being is the realm of the will, of reason, of conscience: the volitional, the rational, the moral. Irving can, therefore, talk of the soul as the seat of righteousness: it has a purely moral capacity.[66] The human soul and its reasoning faculty, is also expressed in terms of conscience: it is the conscience or reason that the Tempter seeks to 'lull asleep'.[67] Alternatively, Irving describes Adam in purely rational terms, 'not reason, neither . . . flesh; but . . . a person endowed with reason, and responsible to God for the right use of the same. Reason and flesh, or in Scriptural language, a living soul'.[68]

Yet however interchangeable Irving's use of the terms soul, reason, and conscience may be, he makes a clear distinction between them and his use of will. Whilst he may use soul and spirit interchangeably when referring to the non-material aspect of human existence, he distinguishes between the two in their relation to reason. The soul refers to the precise location of existence for human being: the will to the power by which all human volition, rationality and morality occur. The 'will is the substance of a spirit, of an intelligent being', so that 'reason without a will, is like a visible world without a sensible creature to possess it'. Therefore, 'the will is before reason, as the sense is before the sensible world'.[64]

We confront here the manner by which Irving expresses the relation between the material and spiritual dimensions of human being: a reasonable will in the soul which moves and controls the physical form of human existence. It is human understanding, the spiritual operating upon natural feeling and bodily sense, the will.[70] Thus Irving asserts:

> The body of man is a noble creature of God, made to rule and command the whole of this visible world . . . These senses were made to possess all material things, and to be possessed by none: the creatures were but the furniture for the entertainment of man's body, and the whole earth was but as the house for it to dwell in; and as the master of the house is more noble than the house, so is the body of man more noble than this earthly tabernacle which it was destined to inherit.[71]

The purely physical aspect of human being thus conforms to the will. The physical conforms to the spiritual: it is a harmony of body and soul, earthly and heavenly. It is also an affirmation of the material dimension to human existence, and a fundamental aspect of Irving's entire doctrine of salvation. In its purely practical dimension, Irving is to be seen no more at his best than when he defends, in an early essay, his philosophy of education within an increasingly industrialized society. Here he argues for an all-embracing education which cultivates the 'common and catholic' against the increasingly specialized. His is a polemic against an increasingly materialistic interpretation of man where human nature is considered to consist 'only of five senses, four lusty limbs, and a voracious body'. It is a plea for 'the old notion' that there is 'a spirit in man, and that the breath of the Almighty hath given him life, that there is a world of faith beyond the world of sight'.[72]

If Irving conceives human being as consisting of 'a reasonable will in the soul which moves and controls the purely material form of human existence,' then in what way is this personal being? Although this is a question he admits not having directed his thought to whilst writing his doctrine of incarnation, nor in the early days of subsequent debate,[73] by 1830 he does address this imbalance in his preface to *The Orthodox And Catholic Doctrine of Our Lord's Human Nature*. Here he distinguishes between the common and the particular in man. The difference between the two is thus:

> Our personality is not given to us by Adam, but by God; and, therefore, we are responsible to God for all the actings of our personal will. But our substance is derived from Adam; we are one substance; with him, though different persons.[74]

The latter is that 'what man was created'. It is the community of the human 'compound nature, body and soul, flesh and reason'.[75] The former is what particularizes each human being. It is 'the individuality or personality, that which we denominate *I myself*; and which God regards as responsible'.[76] Irving arrives at this perspective from his understanding of the incarnation in that the Son did not assume a human person or personality, but came as his very self.[77]

There are interesting theological parallels here: Irving's interpretation of human nature is similar to the way in which he has described the divine identity. That which is both common and particular to Father, Son and Spirit is their community and individuality, respectively. The nearest Irv-

ing comes to expressing an explicit correlation between the
divine and the human in terms of person is in the *Morning
Watch* where human existence is understood as a dynamic
relation in the order of being, after the order of the Trinity.
Notice how Irving attributes the idea of person to the Son:

> The originating fountain of the will doth ever seek to pour itself
> out into the various forms of reason, which all uniting together
> in the personality of a man, constitute what we call *I myself*.
> This is the mystery, of the absolute Godhead expressing itself in
> the unity of Word, or Logos, who is also a person, and properly
> *the Person*, in whom the invisible and incomprehensible sub-
> stance of the Godhead doth body itself into form, for the
> purposes and end of creation.[78]

What is distinctly personal in man is understood to be
distinct from that which is passed on by natural procreation.
The human person is derived from God: it is 'looked on as
holden from God our Creator, and ever responsible to
Him'.[79]

What, then, is the human *person*? It is the responsible
agent. The will is the realm of the personal: 'the personality
standeth in the will'.[80] And this will, the responsible agent,
suggests an Other to whom the human bears responsibility.
Consequently, although in their personal relations human
beings express their individual identities in terms of will, it
also follows that they are wills-in-relation, as beings created
for obedience to their Creator.[81] Our essential humanity is
derived from our relationship with the Creator and obedience to his will. This ultimately reflects the christology
behind Irving's doctrine of human being: the Son who gives
himself in loving obedience to the Father's will in the
economy of salvation.

In summary conclusion, then, to Irving's analysis of
'Paradise Gained', we confront a doctrine of human being
determined by two symbols: the image of God and dominion. Human being is being-with-God, *imago Dei*. It is also
being-in-the-world, *imago mundi*, expressed in dominion
and stewardship. Both are explained within an understanding of will. Through his obedient will, the first Adam is

image bearer. As embodied will, Adam is the *vinculum*, the meeting point between the divine and the created. Human being as image bearer, therefore, is not primarily a statement about the creature, but an expression of our uniqueness within the sphere of creation. In the words of Westermann:

> It is not a declaration about man, but about the creation of man. The meaning can only be understood from what has preceded the creative act. The text is making a statement about an action of God who decides to create man in his image. The meaning must come from the Creation event. What God has decided to create must stand in a relationship to him. The creation of man in God's image is directed to something happening between God and man. The creator created a creature that corresponds to him, to whom he can speak, and who can hear him. It must be noted that man in the Creation narrative is a collective. Creation in the image of God is not concerned with an individual, but with mankind, the species, man. The meaning is that mankind is created so that something can happen between God and man. Mankind is created to stand before God.[82]

## Human Being is in its Becoming: A

> And we all, with unveiled face, beholding the glory of the Lord, are being changed into his likeness from one degree of glory to another; for this comes from the Lord who is the Spirit.[83]

Irving's stress on the will reveals his Western theological context. Human being is distinguished from all other forms of being by virtue of being *imago Dei*. As such, it shares in the same order of being as God. The origin of human existence consists in partaking of divine reality by virtue of intellect and reason.[84] Irving is not wholly rational, however. The human self is not an end in itself. Rather, it finds its meaning in relation to God. Thus, for Irving, the human will designates a hermeneutical rather than merely anthropological concept: it explains what it means to be image bearers of God. We become truly human to the degree we relate to the one who made us.

Secondly, as we relate to the Creator, we move towards

our destiny. We are not created to return to the first Adam's state, however perfect.[85] Rather, our destiny is to be located in what we shall become. The first Adam is perfect as the first of human kind, yet will only be perfected as one who stands in relation to the final destiny of human beings, which, for Irving, is Christ. It is for this reason that understanding of what it means to be human is explained by Irving within his doctrine of Christ. Human being is in its becoming as a type of the incarnate Son, Jesus Christ. Our creation, fall and subsequent redirection are located within the person of the incarnate Son. The full expression of human being, then, is not what is presented in Adam. Rather, it is what we meet in Christ.

It is this emphasis upon the christological dimension of Irving's doctrine of human being that suggests an interesting development of his Western roots. This is no return to Augustine.[86] Rather, Irving continues the Athanasian argument that the Creator's purpose is not thwarted by human infidelity: it is a preparation for the revelation of the Word who reveals to the creature the hidden mind of the Father.[87] Without such a revelation there would be no knowledge of the Creator.[88] Such dependence upon the revealing Word of God permeates Irving's entire thinking: the Son reveals both the divine and the human, and it is revelation for without him there would be no such knowledge.

The development continues in the way Irving parallels Irenaeus' insistence that the human should be created, grow, be strengthened, abound, fall, recover, be glorified, and ultimately see God.[88] Both Irenaeus and Irving stress that to taste of sin is to bring about a greater state of human being: the experience of knowing, then shunning evil, produces a true human character.[90]

Perhaps it is the resonances Irving has with Luther that best reveal how he has developed his theological inheritance. For Luther, Gen.1:20ff is to be understood as showing a distinction between Adam's initial creation and what he was to become. Whilst the first Adam lives a physical life, he is created in order to 'till the ground, not as if he were doing some irksome task and exhausting his body by toil but with supreme pleasure; not as a pastime but in obedience to God

and submission to His will'.[91] Yet, for Luther this is not the
end of creation 'after the physical life was to come a spiritual
life'.[92] This clear distinction between the physical and
spiritual within a continuum leads us to the connection
between Luther and Irving. Both refer to 1 Cor.15:
45–6—' "The first man Adam became a living being"; the
last Adam became a life-giving spirit. But it is not the
spiritual which is first but the physical, and then the
spiritual'. Luther comments thus on this passage:

> The first man was made a 'living soul;' that is, he lived an animal
> life, which needs food, drink, sleep, etc. But 'the second man
> will be renewed into the life-giving spirit'; that is, he will be a
> spiritual man when he reverts to the image of God. He will be
> similar to God in life, righteousness, holiness, wisdom, etc.[93]

It is this antithesis between the first man as living soul, the
physical life, and the last Adam as quickening spirit, that is
of importance to Irving's argument. Even so, he develops it
differently from Luther who distinguishes the first Adam
from the second on the basis of his purely animal-like
existence. Thus, even had Adam not sinned, 'he would still
have lived a physical life in need of food, drink, rest. He
would have grown, procreated, etc., until *he would have
been translated by God to the spiritual life* in which he would
have lived without any animal qualities'.[94]

On the other hand, Irving uses a christological distinction to
distinguish the two. With it we are now able to comment fully
on Irving's doctrine of human being as made in the image of
God. As was outlined above, by virtue of his understanding of
will, Irving is able to suggest that human being is similar in
certain respects to divine being. The boundary of this analogue
is clearly set within a trinitarian setting although 'man was
created in the image of God, he was not so in the same sense in
which Christ is called "the brightness of the Father's glory, and
the express image of His person" '.[95] Irving expands this
distinction in his exegesis of the same passage:

> Adam was not a spiritual creature in the sense in which we are
> spiritual, who are born again of the Spirit by the quickening

power of the Lord Jesus Christ nor was he a creature in the
dignity into which we are adopted by faith . . . Whatever
distinction there is between a soul and spirit,—and such a
distinction there is between the generation of Adam and the
regeneration of Christ.[96]

For Irving, then, the first Adam is identified in terms of soul
in which there is 'a natural incapacity for receiving or
knowing the things which the Spirit teacheth . . . that this is
a form of being preparatory for a higher and more perfect
one, which God might have perhaps have given to our first
parents if they had stood faithful unto Him who created
them. They were perfect in that kind in which they were
created . . . but that kind was not of the perfectest, which
yet awaiteth them, and to which they perhaps would have
been translated if they had not fallen'.[97] In this form of
existence Adam had little knowledge of God beyond that of
Creator. As we have noted earlier, it is only by means of the
revelation of the Father through the Son that human beings
know the true character of God.

Of God's spiritual being I am in great doubt whether he could
have any distinct apprehension or knowledge; because Paul
expressly saith, that the natural man, or the man of the soul, of
which Adam was the perfect form, knoweth not the things of
the Spirit of God: he could not know the Father, who is known
only by the Son, who was not yet come forth from the bosom of
the Father; and not knowing the Son he could not know the
Spirit whose procession succeedeth that of the Son. More than
the knowledge of a Creator he could not have. His being was
only, if I may so speak, preparatory to a spiritual being.[98]

We see, then, that human existence is dynamic and developing, and in so doing complements the trinitarian being of
Father, Son and Spirit. Indeed, the former is derivative of
the latter. Humans make visible the invisible attributes of
pure spirit: both possess understanding, righteousness and
love. In addition, the creation of pure spirit (angelic life) is a
type of embodied spirit (human life). And both are a type of
'that Divine form of being which Christ was to be'.[99] Thus,

the first Adam is a type of the second.[100] Human being, then, has both a horizontal and vertical dimension. Horizontally, it is the fullest creative expression of God: all things point to the arrival of man onto the platform of history. They are but a type of the one who is image bearer. In this being meet the hitherto unrelated dimensions of spirit and matter. But to stop at the optimistic presentation of human being is not merely to misrepresent reality as it now stands, but to belittle the true source and measure of human dignity. This Irving posits within the vertical realm it is in and through our relation of human being to the incarnate Son that we have true worth.

I have discussed above the main criterion by which Irving establishes the value and worth of the human creature. This he locates within the dual appointment to be *imago Dei* and lord of creation. These two aspects contain, in addition, the notions of will and responsibility. With such, Irving constructs his answer to the kind of question posed by Kelsey at the beginning of our chapter. Human beings are able to know God not only by virtue of being image bearers but also due to the fact that, as one of them, God would reveal himself in the person of his Son. By means of his christology, Irving develops an ontology of relations; that is, a means of interpreting reality by means of our relation to God and creation as revealed through Jesus Christ, the incarnate Son. One of the most important aspects of this hermeneutic is the kind of life the human creature can have as a result of such a relational understanding of reality.

The quality of Adam's life is contingent not essential; it is contingent upon being righteous. The will and power to be so are a gift of God.[101] Even life itself is something derived from the Life-giver. This, of course, is hardly a novel assertion. It stands at the very heart of the Adamic story: Adam and Eve are banished from Eden before they could eat from the tree of life. Rather, theirs is a life that receives sustenance from the garden into which they were placed: 'not a life which could have died, not yet a life which could be pronounced immortal'.[102] It is a life complete according to its kind, but not fully perfected. It is incapable of having eternal life.[103] What is of importance here is the way in which Irving combines this interpretation of Genesis with his understanding of human being as being in its becoming. What interests us here is the answer he gives to the second of Kelsey's questions, what is it about human beings that makes fallenness possible in such a radical way as to require the kind of redemption to which Christianity witnesses?

## Master Story 2: Paradise Lost

The Word that expresses what we cannot speak is the living Word that speaks into the deafening silences of exiled humanity from its primal garden. It is the *Deus loquens*, the speaking God, as he participates in the disruption of creation. Yet this reality, as experienced by every subsequent generation of human history, stands starkly against Western doctrines of human being. It sounds indeed, 'strange news from another star'.

It is within this context and against this tension that Irving's significance may be hinted: the christological solution will only be grasped in its relation to his diagnosis of the human predicament.

### Human Being is in its Becoming: B

It is important to contextualize Irving's doctrines of human being and sin. Out of context they appear crude and naïve. At face value the role of sin appears to be over-emphasized. However, Irving is interacting with a very real opponent: the Socinian notion that our present state equals that of the Adamic original.[104] Here Irving reacts against a lighthearted attitude to the eruption of sin into human history. In response, he combats the Socinians by accounting for the fall and the need for salvation in terms that require divine action. Hence his emphasis upon what we may describe as an Irenaean view of creation.

Adam, then, is presented as perfect, but incomplete. Creation cannot have been created perfect in light of both its subsequent demise and the appearance of Christ. Irving argues, 'if the creation had been perfect and sufficient while yet the Christ was unconstituted, then why should there be a Christ at all? There cannot be two perfections, there cannot be two unchangeables, otherwise there were two gods'.[105] Adam is merely the type of Christ: creation in the unfallen state existing only to make way for creation in its fallen state. Consequently, if Adam is understood to be the apex of creation, there can be no divine remedy for a fall: redemption is seen to be a mere after-thought, and no guarantee can be offered in the redeemed state against a further fall.

There is a sense in which, for Irving, Eden is created in order to show the incompleteness of human being. It is preparatory for an even higher state of finite existence. Adam shows that 'the creation, all good though it was, is not the accomplishment but only the beginning of God's purpose'.[106] The goal of creation is outlined in the divine command to refrain from eating the fruit of the tree of the knowledge of good and evil. Although Adam is created with the capacity to have such knowledge, it does not necessarily have to be by disobedience. Irving argues for two consequences of such a state. Firstly that it is a state higher than that of Adam's first condition because it is a knowledge not merely of good, but of good and evil. Secondly, it is a state possessed originally only of God. As such, it can hardly be solely an evil state: it must be a state capable of being attained by means other than that of disobedience. Humankind must have been able to attain such a state through obedience. Whatever the case, it is clear that human beings *become* through a process of development.

Irving combines this notion of maturation with our ultimate destiny through the way in which he perceives God to have united himself with his creation. This notion of union is one that surfaces in Irving's thought in two pivotal areas: his doctrines of God and creation. The original creation was one utterly distinct from its Creator, with little or no knowledge of spiritual life or Fatherly love. In its primal state, the creation does not reflect its final goal. Rather,

> a creation out of God was not the ultimate end of the purpose, but a creation united to God, and yet not mixed with him,

through the union of a creature redeemed with the manhood taken into the person of the Son.[107]

We return to his central concern: creation and human being have meaning solely in and through the incarnate Son. Despite its original perfection—the trees of life and knowledge of good and evil; the sufficiency of all desires; the completeness of all power; perfect love, and harmony of companionship; the presence and manifestation of God—'the trees of his planting, the woman of his creating, and Satan of his permitting'[108]—the perfection of creation rests not in the greatest expression of divine fiat, the human creature, but in the incarnation of the Son. Indeed, this act of the Son by the Father through the Spirit is intimately associated with the development of human being in its becoming that which the Creator intends. It is, however, a becoming not by a return to any original perfection. This would be a retrograde step: it would cast doubt on the Creator's ability to maintain his creation. Therefore, in what way and by what means does the Creator bring about his desired goal? To answer this we must explore Irving's understanding of sin.

## The Act

We move from the primary state of human being, of simple goodness, to the second, the fall, the state of the knowledge of good and evil, through disobedience.

> It was necessary that Adam should pass into a fallen state, to shadow forth Christ in the fallen state, and to this very end was paradise created with all its ordinances.[109]

It is within this second state of creation that the uniting action of God is seen in an alternative mode of action, for it is a divine motivation towards an alienated creation. It is the action of the triune Creator, and especially of the Father out of love for his creation, pursuing it into its far country in order not only to reconcile it to himself, but in so doing to bring it into its fullest and most perfect expression through the incarnate Son.

As has been hinted, the fall of Adam does not take the Creator by surprise, yet neither is it a predetermined and necessary act on the creature's part. It does not thwart the Creator's intentions. Rather, it is an act of human 'disobedience both known and foreseen, and permitted by God'.[110] Indeed, the introduction of human disobedience into the scene of history is necessary 'as a part of the great scheme'.[111] There is, obviously, a somewhat nervous tension between the necessity of sin on the one hand with the preclusion of divine culpability on the other. Irving appears to be aware of this tension but far from allowing it into his doctrine of God, he uses it to show how the full grace and love of God can be revealed.

So, how can he suggest that sin is necessary, whilst maintaining God is not responsible for it? This is a question Irving does not address directly, so that he does appear to jeopardize his position. It is a fair criticism until we consider the two different but complementary perspectives by which he approaches the fall. Theologically, he defends God from any culpability on the grounds that both the original freedom of uncaused human will, and the exalted position of human being as the link between creation and God, safeguard his theodicy, his explanation for the existence of sin and evil. Teleologically, that is, in terms of the ultimate goal, although God cannot be responsible for the fall, he permits it in order to fulfil his plan for creation. It may be more helpful to interpret the language of necessity on Irving's part in terms of permission, that is, a fall or not, the sovereign will of the Creator is not thwarted due to the fact that his ultimate will for the perfection of creation lies outside that creation in the Son who reveals the Father. Without these two considerations, Irving is not only misrepresented but can be interpreted as making sin an end in itself. This is not the case. From his very earliest writings he states the context within which talk of sin should be made:

The Fall is not an origin—the creation is before it: and the purpose of God in Christ is before creation, and is the true origin of all being, the true end of all revelation.[112]

We can detect two different but complementary perspectives concerning the way in which Irving approaches the idea of the fall. Negatively, the fall is permitted in order to distinguish the Creator from the creature, as well as affirm the order of relations that exist between the two.

In order . . . to preserve distinctness between the invisible and absolute God and the visible limited creature, it was necessary that the creature should fall: and, by falling, should know the end and inferiority that is in itself; and that the goodness which it had originally, is a goodness derived from another source than itself, seeing there hath not been, in itself, the power of retaining it.[113]

Yet Irving is also at pains to show that sin is not the creation of God: it comes about by the uncaused and free will of the creature.[114] It is a condition of the creature which reveals how inferior the creature is to the Creator.[115]

In addition, Irving understands the fall to have been permitted in order to bring about a higher form of existence. As we have noted above, it brings the creature into a knowledge of good and evil. But it also initiates the human creature to be the bearer of God's wrath against sin. Although the inner image is deformed and the body, the outer form, destined to death, human being remains accountable for its capacity as image bearer since it has not been immediately consumed as a result of sin. If it were so, human being would be a 'monument of wrath consumed' rather than a 'free-will actor of God's wrath'.[116] It is the God-given capacity to overcome sin, and in so doing to declare God's sentence upon it, that affirms the dignity of human being even in its fallen state.[117]

Positively, Irving understands the fall of Adam as preparatory to the arrival of the God-man onto the stage of human history.[118] If there were no fall, we would have no knowledge of the Son, neither in his offices as prophet, priest and king, nor in his names as Jesus, Christ and Lord. Consequently, 'the fall is as essential for giving the God-man His dignity over and above the creatures, as it is for teaching the creature its distinctness from the invisible and incomprehensible Godhead'.[119]

In response to a question whether God's purposes could have been achieved without a fall, Irving is hesitant, except to say that 'this was the best way of accomplishing it'.[120] Thus he states that, 'while I assert the necessity of sin as a part of the great scheme, I wholly disallow that any creature was made for sin, but every creature for Christ'.[121] The salient point here is that Irving approaches the problem of sin and its eruption into a previously perfect context not in the light of sin, but of Christ, for 'the end of creation was the Christ'. But he also implies an inherent necessity to sin, for he goes on to say, 'this is the great end and purpose of sin in the creation of God, which, if you consider it well, is as essential to the fulness of the scheme, as is creation itself'.[122] This necessity is subsumed within his doctrine of election, both universal and particular. It is not central to our discussion, but highlights the fact that Irving does not deal with sin as an end in itself but always in its relation to God's intention in incarnation. Whilst his stress upon the necessity of sin may appear somewhat deterministic, it stems from the stress he places on the appearance of Christ, as well as the importance he places upon the relatedness between the creature and the Creator. It is within this context, therefore, that he resolves the 'nervous tension' between his seemingly incompatible approach to sin when he concludes his article on 'God's method and order of revealing himself' in *Morning Watch*:

> What we behold is not a creation destroyed, an idea of God marred or defeated; but it is a creation growing into that stable form in which it existed from the beginning in the Divine *idea*. Sin hath disclosed to man the guilt of a sinner, and taught him the dependence of a creature, and declared the mercy and grace of God; but it hath not interfered with God's original design of bringing a creature which should come to its glory through the way of death, as Christ cometh to his glory through the same. He would have done, and could have done it without sin and suffering to man by the ordinance of the forbidden tree, which

was in effect the same prostration of the creature; but man would have the other way, of knowing good and evil, and he hath got it: but the end it plan, and the course of God is the same, and every defalcation in his creature only revealeth new funds of Divine excellency in the Creator; and so we shall see it to be unto the end.[123]

## The Diagnosis

Adam's act of disobedience, historicized in the Genesis account of the fall, brings about a dislocation in human being: he is no longer the image of God. Nor is he the creature who speaks on behalf of God. He does not embody the truth. Rather, in the primal act of disobedience, the truth is exchanged for a lie and humanity becomes untrue to its true self. Adam, created to be holy and righteous, denudes himself of his true inheritance as lord of creation. His suffering and death become a lie against an intended order, for having lied 'upon God'[124] he has betrayed that for which he was created. As a result, human being is no longer capable of expressing the fulness of God's image or of being his vice-regent.

Adams untruth does not, however, create any thing or creature. The lie of human being is illuminated only by the light of true human being, the incarnate Lord. However, since God alone is Creator, the lie cannot be a created thing with a life of its own. It is, rather, the parasitic resistance of a free creature against its creator. The fallen condition, then for Irving, is but 'the evil . . . condition of creation, proceeding from the freedom of the will of man, who was invested with creation's weal or creation's woe'.[125] It is a state of being 'the *state* of a creature,—the second state of a creature'.[126]

What is this state? It is the state of sin. The horror of the first act that brings about this new state is revealed in its consequences. It is an 'eternal and unchangeable . . . condition' into which the human will is brought. It is an alienation of the will from its proper disposition: 'a spiritual act against a Spirit, against the good and gracious Father of spirits'.[127] This emphasis on the will as the seat of sin, and the identification of will with spirit, supports Irving's insistence upon the direct consequences of the fall that were only overcome in Christ. We can see the relationship between will and spirit more clearly when Irving addresses the angelic fall, a fall from a purely spiritual state of existence, where he insists there can be no reconstruction of the former state of relations with the divine: there is no higher created state than the spiritual. Indeed, as Coleridge later comments, 'if it be hard to explain how Adam fell; how much more hard to solve how purely spiritual beings could fall?'.[128] Yet such a state is not the destiny of embodied spirit. What hope, however, is there for 'the will of a spirit which of its own accord hath swerved away, which did not choose to stand when all was in its favour?'[129] None, he insists. A revelation of divine omnipotence is, of itself, unable to bridge the chasm created by Adam's action. Consequently, Irving's entire thrust is to show how the human predicament may be resolved only by 'the revelation of more persons than one in the Godhead'.[130] It comes as no surprise, then, that he interprets the Son's work as that of redeeming the human will from its self-inflicted bondage.

Irving identifies two forms of sin. What he calls 'actual sin' is sin performed by the human person when yielding to the sinful disposition in human nature.[131] This is the act of a spirit or will against the one who is pure Spirit. However, it is with the second form, that of original sin, that Irving is particularly concerned when tackling the relationship between the human condition and its solution in Christ. He addresses this most specifically in his later treatise, *Christ's Holiness in Flesh*, in which he is at pains to shed light upon the kind of humanity assumed by the Son in incarnation.

*Unde malum faciamus*—whence comes the fact that we sin? Irving locates the answer in the doctrine of original sin which he approaches from two complementary perspectives. Firstly, he incorporates the theological motif of 'original sin' within his doctrine of Christ. If the Son assumes his incarnate form by means of supernatural, not ordinary, generation, and is guilty of neither 'actual' nor 'original' sin, then there are two possible corollaries. Firstly, original sin tells us something about the human person. It is a state *in* which the human person is born by virtue of natural conception. Irving qualifies this elsewhere by insisting that conception by natural means is not the 'cause of our original guiltiness in God's sight'. Rather, 'it is the *sign and seal* of God's will and purpose . . . that we should be so concluded sinful and helpless in ourselves, to the end we might be introduced into the knowledge of his grace'.[132] But this is not a state into which the Son is born. Christ is guiltless of original sin due to the fact of his virgin birth. He is not an individual like other sinful individuals because 'He is not a human person He never had personal subsistence as a mere man'.[133] Secondly, it has to do with the humanly generated matter *into* which the embodied human person is born. 'It is sin', he concludes, 'to be born as we are through ordinary generation', and by 'sin' he means original sin.[134] But what does this sin mean for subsequent heirs to Adam's lot?

To answer this, we turn to the other of Irving's perspectives on original sin. Here he focuses attention on the implications of Adam as the origin of human being. Irving refers to Adam's original state of innocence as a means of qualifying the meaning of 'original sin'. If the creation of all human beings stands in Adam, that is, in him all human beings find their origin, created good and accountable for that good, then there is a collective solidarity responsible for this first act of disobedience and its consequences. For Irving, this represents one pole of human nature; our solidarity, our unity by virtue of descending from the first Adam. All humanity is implicated in the guilt of Adam's sin. The other pole of humanity is its diversity which Irving identifies as our personality: that for which each individual is held responsible for the actions performed in the body.[135] But it is in light of the initial origin, of having been created in original righteousness, that the subsequent state of original sin finds its meaning.

Original sin is the state into which every human person comes to be as a result of Adam's primal act of disobedience by virtue of natural conception and generation. The character of original sin is reflected in the fact that it is both a state to which each human being contributes by 'actual sin' and a state which is 'already there'.[136] To quote Ricoeur:

The Adamic myth reveals at the same time this mysterious aspect of evil, namely, that if any one of us initiates evil, inaugurates it . . . each of us also *discovers evil*, finds it already there, in himself, outside himself, and before himself . . . For every consciousness which awakens when responsibility is taken, evil is *already there*. In tracing back the origin of evil to a distant ancestor, the myth discovers the situation of every man: evil has already taken place. I do not begin evil; I continue it. I am implicated in evil.[137]

The sense of discovering sin as 'already there' can be seen in the mortality of infants long before any act by a disobedient will. This is an important point in his argument against the idea that each individual is 'in as good and perfect a state as Adam, and as able to keep the law as he was'.[138] Rather, it is suffering and death that prove the human creature to be fallen, and therefore distinct from Adam's original state. Remove such a criterion and the distinction between fallen and unfallen is lost. Original sin denotes, therefore, the collective solidarity of the human race, the collective state into which we are all born. It stands, therefore, 'in our having been created otherwise than we now are born'.[139]

It is the confession to our being created by a holy God, to our becoming guilty by our own act, to our needing a Redeemer; and it is the seal of our unity as a family, as one stock and one substance.[140]

## The Consequences

They cannot scare me with their empty spaces
Between stars—on stars where no human race is.
I have it in me so much nearer home
To scare me with my own desert places.[141]

The search today for meaningful human identity has become a babel of conflicting and relativized stories amidst the increasing chaos and insecurity that has become the hallmark of our time. As we reach out to extend the boundaries of our knowledge and dominion, we appear to become more fragmented and alienated from the richness and profusion promised in the Eden mandate: to have dominion and prosper. It is into this context that Irving speaks, a context embraced within the Genesis story of Eden and exile, of paradise and wilderness. The Genesis presentation of creation with its order of relations, in which human beings are placed to be lord and from which they subsequently fall with catastrophic results, is no fable. Such a story expresses most eloquently the human predicament.

As a result of some kind of fall, human being is no longer the embodied spirit which lives creatively as *imago Dei* and *imago mundi*, as one created and called to exist in that creative tension of both spirit and matter. It no longer knows the dynamic freedom of realizing all the possibilities for which it was created. It becomes grounded in its own fallenness and predilection to sinning against its Creator, self and environment. As a result, the intended blessings for humanity are exchanged for a 'desert place'. The structure of relations with God, self and creation are exchanged for a lie. Ultimately, the dislocation brought about in our demise presumes 'false shadows for true substances'.[142] Within this context, Irving's stress upon the immediacy of the Genesis story is a call to remembrance, for, he advocates,

> the truth is that men have forgotten what the fall was and how really it is now to be perceived in every thing, without exception, pertaining to the age that is now . . . It is not that he who suffereth sickness hath therefore peculiarly sinned; but it is that sickness stands as the visible expression of the corruption of sin.[143]

## God-ward

Irving is adamant that the fall of Adam does not take God unawares. Adam exists in the context of perfect relations: with Creator, partner and domain over which he exercises his lordship and expresses his creativity. He is not left alone in the garden, but is visited by and communes with the Creator. The benefits of these relations are ruptured by the first act of disobedience. Sin is interpreted as an act of eternal consequence. Sin cannot be separated from its result: it is not a thing in itself. As Irving retorts to the notion that the two can be separated, as in Arminian thinking, ' "Hate the sin, but love the sinner." What mean they? that sin is something by itself, and the sinner something by himself, so distinct from one another, that the one may well be hated, and the other may well be loved?'[144] Not so for Irving: sin is not something to be downplayed. Rather, not only is the person the sinner but 'the substance, the dominion which these persons possess, are also sinful'.[145]

In order to assert that the fall does not take God by surprise, Irving returns to his christology. Firstly, God creates man in such a manner that if he were to fall, there should be a way of return. The soulish, earthly existence of the first Adam is but preparatory for the spiritual and more perfect second Adam.[146] But this perception of human existence only has significance in light of the anterior christological belief that such an event of falling has already been accounted for. In order to establish this foundation Irving unpacks his understanding of Christ's sacrifice. Creation is not an end in itself. Its meaning is derived from its Creator's purpose. This is the force behind Irving's entire argument. He is not content to focus solely upon God's gracious action in atonement for sin. This, for Irving, is only of secondary importance. Rather, the primary point is how one may defend against committed sin.[147] Irving finds such a defence in his understanding of Christ as 'the Lamb slain before the foundation of the world' (Revelation 13:8). As such, sacrifice is prior in ontological order to creation, that is, it precedes it both in priority and chronology. Its full importance is found not merely in an event within history, but as a consideration 'proper to God himself . . . (who) is in the essence of His being the Holy One, who cannot be controverted or contradicted, and hath no indulgence of sin whatever'. Consequently, the Creator himself takes account of any subsequent sin.

> Abhorrence of sin, and destruction to it, is the way of death, is an indefeasible constitution of the Godhead, ratified and made sure before creation, in order to be creation's beacon against sin.[148]

Although human sin has real consequences, the Creator is not impotent, nor are his intentions thwarted. More importantly, when sin arose in the mind of man, although serious as an act against the constitution of God, it was also an act which God had 'already realized and declared' by virtue of the Son's obedience to be the slain Lamb.[149]

## Self-ward

The light of the divine word brings sin into view. What does the Christian understand by sin? Sin is primarily a metaphysical phenomenon whose roots lie in the mystic depths of man's spiritual nature. The essence of sin consists not in the infringement of ethical standards but in a falling away from the divine eternal life for which man was made and to which, by his very nature, he is called. Sin is committed first of all in the secret depths of the human spirit but its consequences distort the whole individual. A sin will reflect on a man's psychological and physical condition, on his outward appearance, on his personal destiny. Sin will, inevitably, pass beyond the boundaries of the sinner's own life to burden all humanity and thus affect the fate of the whole world. The sin of our forefather Adam was not the only sin of cosmic significance. Every sin, secret or manifest, committed by each one of us, has a bearing on the rest of the universe.[150]

Irving stands resolutely within the stream of Christian tradition which, here expressed by the Archimandrite, asserts that a radical inversion of human being has occurred. Alongside the *noblesse* of human being exists the pitiable squalor of its brokenness. Hope may well spring eternal in the human breast, according to Arnold, but it is a hope all too tarnished by our common lot, for it is our lot to become the food of worms. We strive heavenward to transcend our earthbound existence like condemned creatures, too willing to exchange one cage for another in the hope of gaining rest from or for our restless spirits.

Irving's favourite allusion for expressing the human plight is the story of Aeschylus' Prometheus. Here he finds expressed the present bondage of the human will. Prometheus, identified with Adam, is a soul that was once free but has come into bondage and is assailed by tormentors. For Irving, Prometheus represents the high dignity of humanity in its refusal to give in utterly to the dark forces of the purely earthly and material. He is a presentation of the human soul facing torment and temptation who holds out in hope of a better form of live. Prometheus is the 'will enduring the bondage of all the creation, and groaning within itself, waiting for the redemption of the body, and meanwhile saved by hope, and in the strength of that hope preferring its bondage to all the power and liberty which is contained within the bounds of creation under its present laws'.[151] What is in captivity? The human will. To what is it in bondage? The oppression of the devil, the world and the flesh. What is the redemption? The deliverance of the human will from its bondage.[152]

Irving explains the dynamics of sin both in terms of our place within creation and in relation to the human will. The former explains how Adam's sin brings about a new state of being. It is a fall from the highest and most noble of human parts, the personality.[153] Through the person sin enters the mind, takes hold of the body, and then through the body to those creatures placed to serve him, until through them to the earth itself.[154] In this manner, Adam loses his lordship to that which has authority over him, and expresses itself through his physical existence.

By our will, on the other hand, Irving denotes how the true order of being has been inverted. The result is a drastic reversal in the way the human will operates. Whilst Adam relates in obedience to his Creator there is harmony not only between God and Adam, but also between human will and body, reason and understanding. However, the act of disobedience reverses such relationships. No longer is Adam able to respond in his will and reason to the divine will. Rather, his will is enslaved to his understanding, natural feelings or bodily senses. Consequently, God's revelation to embodied spirit no longer meets with or relates to the entire person, but merely to 'different parts of the natural man'. There results not only a bondage of will but a blindness in spiritual perception, for God's revelation becomes restricted to the senses, feelings or understanding. For Irving, then, bondage of the will represents a falling into a state of pure immanence: a state of existence in which human life is bound to the purely physical, animal and material.[155]

## Creation-ward

Perhaps we detect just how modern Irving is when we turn to his understanding of our human responsibility for the world around us. His doctrine of human being suggests some very helpful pointers towards engaging with the contemporary ecological debate. Our present world-view with its blatant denial of an established order of being with clear boundaries may be understood as a modern expression of the diabolical. The outcome of our erroneous cosmology confronts us, eventually, with the stark reality that even our world itself has become something it was never intended to become.

It is clear that ecological concerns are self-defeating unless we show that there is a reason for giving the non-human order significance and meaning.[156] Irving locates this foundation in the theological implications of the Genesis story with the creation mandate that Adam is both to prosper and have dominion. With this he seeks to establish a world-view that affirms the created order, and does it by unpacking what it means for creation to derive its value from its Creator. Firstly, the human creature derives value from being both the image bearer of God and the lord of creation. In this we are called into partnership of vice-regency with the supreme Lord God. Secondly, and as a corollary of this, creation itself stands or falls with its appointed lord, the human creature. It derives its order of being from the quality of life possessed by man. In the fall, the 'fine gold of Adam's dust'[157] is exchanged for a lie and when this is done, creation is denied its two great desires: to see God and to be able to name his name by virtue of its created lord.[158] Consequently, rather than being the idyllic setting for human innocence and growth, 'the world, by the first transgression, hath become the free stage for the controversy between good and evil'.[159] What is so positive about Irving's view is the fact that he interprets this fall from the perspective of the

Creator's final goal. When Adam falls he does not fall into total isolation from his Creator. Although he comes to know and experience sin, it is a knowledge that is itself contained within the canopy of God's grace and sovereignty. Adam falls from one state into another, what Irving calls 'the gospel by the promise', namely, that 'he, and all his children . . . should exercise faith and hope upon Him that was to come'.[160]

The fall, then, acts as a preparation for what is to come: Adam, the living soul, falls into the earthly in order that he may be lifted up to the spiritual.[161] And he will do so in relation to the incarnate Son.[162]

This christological emphasis pervades Irving's entire doctrine of human being. Human being is in its becoming: in its becoming conformed to the image of the image of God. It is because of his understanding of Christ that Irving seeks to explain the coming together of God and man in the incarnation. What is of importance for both Parts I and II is the fact that whilst Christ is unequivocally central to his entire theology, Irving perceives both the human and the divine aspects of incarnation as held together by virtue of the Spirit. That is, there is a profound pneumatic element to Irving's theology. The significance of this is not to be missed and we shall explore this in detail in Part III. However, Irving does not allow it to dictate his perception of Jesus Christ: at all times, the subject of the Christ-event is the eternal Son of God, who is the object of hope excercized and anticipated by fallen creation.

And now . . . all heaven and earth looked forward for the Man, by eminancy called THE SON OF MAN; that is, the child for whom manhood was created, and through whom the great secret was to be revealed, and the Divine nature for ever manifested in an outward form;- which was, as it were, the great deliverance for which the womb of all creation had longed, and made an empty and abortive effort to produce it at the birth of Adam, when things were not yet ripe for the great discovery . . . It was the purpose and decree of God, promulgated from the foundation of the world, and gradually growing into manifestation by slow degree and manifold pangs of creation, according to the importance, the infinite and all-comprehending importance, of the issues which rested with it. For . . . the nucleus of the whole scheme, the great end and first beginning of all and that which appears above the earth, or the preparing of the soil for the casting of the seed into the earth. And so God, and angels, and men, and devils, and whatever else existeth, all looked forward to the Man in whose outward form the Godhead was to become eternally manifest. For that in man it was to be manifest, God himself had purposed from all eternity; and the angels, no doubt, had heard the rumour of it; wherefore the morning stars sang together, and the angels of God shouted at His birth: and Satan, with his apostacy, had also heard a rumour of it, wherefore he solicited Him with his wiles to forsake His allegiance and the knowledge was kept alive, amongst the sons of men, by every revelation made to the patriarchs and the prophets; until at length in Bethlehem, in the stable of Bethlehem—fit emblem of the world into which He was born—the child of infinite hopes and longings was brought into being: whereupon instantly the heavenly host waked all their choral symphonies, and sang, 'Glory to God in the highest; peace on earth, and good will to the children of man'.[162]

# Footnotes

[1] Tertullian, *On the Flesh of Christ*, The Ante-Nicene Fathers, vol.III, Buffalo: The Christian Literature Publishing Co, 1885, 530.

[2] 1 John 1:1,3.

[3] K Ware, 'The Unity of Human Person According to the Greek Fathers' in *Persons and Personality. A Contemporary Inquiry*, eds. A Peacocke, G Gillet, Oxford: Basil Blackwell Ltd, 1987, 197–206.

[4] J Calvin, *Institutes of the Christian Religion*, 1.1.1, Philadelphia: The Westminster Press, 1960, 35.

[5] K Barth, *Church Dogmatics*, 3.2, Edinburgh: T & T Clark, 1960, 73.

[6] See DW Dorries' unpublished doctoral thesis, *Nineteenth Century British Christological Controversy, Centring Upon Edward Irving's Doctrine of Christ's Human Nature*. University of Aberdeen, 1987. Dorries presents overwhelming evidence from Patristic through Reformation thought to show that Irving's doctrine of the humanity of Christ is consistent with what preceded him and accepted as orthodox. Although at times Dorries pushes his data to imply more than the writers are themselves saying his thesis is a step forward in Irving research and one that establishes both the orthodoxy and credibility of

Irving's christology, as well as show how misrepresented and misunderstood was his thinking.

7   DH Kelsey, *Christian Theology*, eds. P Hodgson, R King, London: SPCK, 1983, 141.

8   Taken from the title of a story by Herman Hesse, *Merkwürdige Nachrich von einem andern Stern, Strange News from Another Star & Other Tales*, trans. J Wright, New York: Farrar, Strava & Grox, 1972.

9   Cited in DJ Hall, *Imaging God: Dominion as Stewardship*, Grand Rapids: Wm B Eerdmans Publishing Co., 1986, 204.

10  See footnote 4.

11  CW1, 73–74.

12  *op cit*, 331.

13  CS Lewis, *God in the Dock*, Glasgow: William Collins' Sons & Co Ltd, 1979, 31. Lewis' sentiments reiterate those of seventh century Leontius of Cyprus, 'Creation does not venerate the Maker through itself directly, but it is through me that the heavens declare the glory of God, through me the moon worships God, through me the stars glorify him, through me the waters and showers of rain, the dew and all creation, venerate God and give him glory.' *PG*, XCIII, 1604B. Cited in Ware, *op cit*, 204.

14  CHF, 116.

15  *op cit*, 14.

16  MW7, 52.

17  CHF, 116.

18  MW7, 60.

19  MW5, 386.

20  CW5, 239.

21  *ibid*.

22  PW2, 151.

23  SE Alsford, *Sin as a problem of Twentieth Century Systematic Theology*, unpublished PhD thesis, University of Durham, 282.

24  PW2, 411.

25  *op cit*, 382.

26  TF Torrance, *Calvin's Doctrine of Man*, London: Lutterworth Press, 1952, 80.

27  See AI McFadyen, *The call to personhood*, for a detailed presentation of personhood as a response to the invitation of the other which 'calls' us into true relationship.

28  *op cit*, 80.

29  OG, 78.

30  MW5, 387.

31  *op cit*, 388.

32  K Barth, *Church Dogmatics*, III.1, 183ff.

33  PW2, 12. Note the similarity with Eastern interpretations of human being, for instance, Theophilus of Antioch:

Man is in his nature neither mortal nor immortal. If he had been from the beginning created immortal he would have been as God. On the other hand, if he had been created mortal then it follows that God would have been responsible for his death. Therefore he was not created either mortal or immortal, but capable of either. (*Ad Autolycum* 11.27).

Cited in N El-Khoury, 'Anthropological Concepts in the School of Antioch' in *Studia Patristica*, XVII, Part II, ed. EA Livingstone, Oxford: Pergamon Press, 1982, 1359–1365, 1363.

[34] CHF, 116.
[35] MW7, 60.
[36] MW5, 388.
[37] *ibid*.
[38] CHF, 14.
[39] *ibid*.
[40] CHF, 104.
[41] PW1, 313.
[42] CHF, 20.
[43] *op cit*, 14. See also M Gervase, *Byzantine Aesthetics*, 23. Cited in AM Allchin, *Sacrament & Image*, (introduction), Fellowship of St. Alban & St Sergius 2nd edn., 1987.

Because man is body he shares in the material world around him, which passes within him through his sense perceptions. Because man is mind he belongs to the world of higher reality and pure spirit. Because he is both, he is, in Cyril of Alexandria's phrase, 'God's crowned image'; he can mould and manipulate the material and make it articulate.

[44] CHF, 39.
[45] *op cit*, 20.
[46] CW5, 454.
[47] MW7, 54.
[48] PW2, 413.
[49] Hall, *op cit*, 127, 132.
[50] PW2, 412.
[51] MW7, 63.
[52] MW7, 62.
[53] PW2, 382.
[54] *ibid*.
[55] Similar sentiments are expressed in TF Torrance, 'The Goodness and Dignity of Man in the Christian Tradition', *Modern Theology* 4:4, 1988, 309–322.
[56] CHF, 20.
[57] CW5, 449.
[58] *Lectures on the Book of Revelation*, London: Baldwin and Craddock, 1829, Lecture 1, 51.
[59] MW7, 60.
[60] *op cit*, 61.

[61] JM Boulger, *Coleridge As Religious Thinker*, New Haven: Yale University Press, 1961, 225–226.

[62] See E TeSelle, *Christ in Conflict. Divine Purpose & Human Possibility*, Philadelphia: Fortress Press, 1975.

[63] *ibid*, 118.

[64] PW1, 345.

[65] CW1, 538.

[66] CHF, 104.

[67] CW1, 218. See also, PW1, 333.

[68] PW2, 209.

[69] CW5, 425.

[70] *op cit*, 52.

[71] CW1, 221.

[72] *Extracts From a Sermon on Education*, (preached 1825). Glasgow: Maurice Ogle & Sons, 1854, 27.

[73] OCD, ix.

[74] CW2, 538.

[75] OCD, ix.

[76] *ibid*.

[77] Irving makes no distinction between the two. MW7, 60–61. This will be discussed in the following chapter which will focus purely on Irving's christology.

[78] MW7, 60–61.

[79] PW2, 209.

[80] CHF, 63.

[81] See J Macmurray, *The Self As Agent*, London: Faber and Faber Limited, 1957, *Persons in Relation*, London: Faber and Faber Limited, 1961. Macmurray criticizes Kantian and post-Kantian perceptions of 'person' in ways that parallel Irving. Error in theory results in failure in practice, our misconception of what it means to be a person can lead only to a misconception of our own reality, (PR, 149). The 'person' is not derived from a science of mind, but by agency. It is practical, (SA, 62–85). Macmurray argues for an understanding of personhood in terms of self-as-agent and self-as-subject, incorporating the bodily and mental aspects of human existence. Whilst both appear to be mutually exclusive they are of pivotal importance in describing what it is to be a human person. In PR Macmurray seeks to transfer the centre of human reference away from the mind to the body as a means of affirming the personal, (12). In so doing, there is a shift from the solely subjective and negative self-as-agent. The ego-entrapped thinker becomes 'person' in relation to other embodied, thinking beings. Thus, Macmurray stands in the same tradition as Irenaeus, Luther and Irving in his assertion that human personhood comes about through the rhythm of 'withdrawal and return', (86–105). Human personhood does not exist 'at an instant' but is the ongoing product of action generated in time. It is the process of personal development, of human effort in discerning what is good and bad, real or false, (107–8). The ultimate questions are concerned about whether

what is exists, is personal or not. And for there to be a personal ontology there must be a personal God.

82  C Westermann, *Creation*, trans. JJ Scullion, Philadelphia: Fortress Press, 1974, 56. Cited in Hall, op cit, 73.

83  2 Corinthians 3:18.

84  See *Sermon on Education*, op cit, 8. Here Irving outlines the three original capacities of the soul, held by all human beings to greater or lesser degrees. Firstly, there is scientific knowledge and understading whereby we know and understand the natural world by means of our five senses as explored and examined by our understanding. Secondly, there is personal knowledge: the capacity for self-understanding, conscience, moral judgement, psychology, social relations of family and government, all of which Irving identifies as 'all that inward activity of spirit, and outward condition of life, which distinguishes man from the lower creatures' (8). Thirdly, there is spiritual knowledge, 'the power of knowing and worshipping, and obeying the true God'. Only a form of education which gives place and dignity to each of these respective areas of human activity and knowledge is 'liberal, catholic and complete' (8).

85  CW5, 322.

86  See CE Gunton *The One, The Three and the Many*.

87  Athanasius, *The Incarnation of the Word of God*, London: Geoffrey Bles, The Centenery Press, 1944, 8§54, 93.

88  op cit, 3§11, 37–38.

89  Irenaeus, *Against Heresies*, IV.xxviii.3, Ante-Nicene Christian Library, vol.v, Edinburgh: T&T Clark, 1880.

90  op cit, III.xx.2, IV.xxxix.2, V.iii.1.

91  Luther, *Commentary on Genesis*, XLII, Saint Louis: Concordia Publishing House, 1958, 48–49.

92  ibid.

93  ibid.

94  op cit, 65–66, 86.

95  CW5, 80.

96  CW5, 81.

97  ibid.

98  CW5, 82.

99  CW5, 93.

100 See *Ben Ezra*, ccxxxff for a detailed outline of Christ as Prophet, Priest and King. Also, CW5, 81.

101 CS, 13.

102 MW7, 302.

103 CW5, 416.

104 An anti-trinitarian group started by the Italian, Faustus Pavolo Sozzini (1539–1604) who believed humanity to be mortal by nature. Eternal life is a gift from God for the righteous who alone will be resurrected. Sozzini believed Christ not to be divine by nature but only by virtue of his offices: divinity can be attributed to him, but not divine nature. Thus, the doctrine of the three offices of Christ

(Prophet, Priest and King) is central to Socinian theology and one which Irving vehemently defends in terms of divine nature, and not divinity alone. Harnack summarizes the Socinian doctrine of Christ as that in which 'Christ has perfectly revealed to us the divine will' (*History of Dogma*, vol.VII, London: Williams & Norgate, 1988, 118–167).

[105] CW5, 98.

[106] MW7, 63.

[107] MW7, 63.

[108] MW7, 64.

[109] ibid.

[110] CW5, 10.

[111] CW5, 103.

[112] LD, 499.

[113] CW5, 419. See also CW5, 239.

[114] CW5, 10.

[115] CW5, 99, 239.

[116] PW2, 153.

[117] This is only a possibility because there is an order of being prior to that of creation, namely, sacrifice. It is because creation has its being and meaning in and through the Lamb slain before the creation of the world that not only is sin already accounted for in its relation to a holy Creator, but the character of God is vindicated before any violation or offence occurs.

[118] CW5, 91.

[119] CW5, 423.

[120] CW5, 203.

[121] CW5, 103.

[122] CW5, 98.

[123] MW5, 394. Italics mine. Note that this is not a return to the original form, but to the original will of the Creator.

[124] OCLHN, 63.

[125] PW2, 405.

[126] CW5, 218.

[127] CW5, 18.

[128] ST Coleridge, *Literary Remains*, vol.3, London: William Pickering, 1883, 330.

[129] CW5, 18.

[130] ibid.

[131] OCD, x.

[132] OCD, 84–85.

[133] CW5, 159.

[134] CHF, 3.

[135] CHF, 56.

[136] See footnote 23 for 'tensive symbol'. P Ricoeur, 'Origial Sin:' A Study in Meaning', in *The Conflict of Interpretations. Essays in Hermenutics*, ed. D Thole, Evanston: Northwestern University Press, 1974. Sin is a rational symbol declaring the radical nature of sin. It is more true to

say that sin is something which 'inhabits' human being than to say that human being 'commits' sin (238). It is interesting to note how Irving and Ricoeur give similar meaning to the mysterious aspect of evil, to the dual character of sin: that we inaugurate evil (actual sin) but also find it (original sin).

[137]    Ricoeur, 238. Like Irving, Ricoeur asserts that 'sin is not a something, but a subversion of a relation', 'The Hermeneutics of Symbols:1', op cit, 303. Both denounce any attempt to belittle the significance of sin by suggesting its 'non-being'. It has being in that it is the subversion of an intended objective reality, a reality which refuses to be thwarted by sin, but overcomes only by grace. It is in light of both Irving and Ricoeur's interpretation of sin, both acutal and original, inaugurated and found, that any dulling between human nature and personhood in relation of the saving work of Christ is contested. If we proclaim humanity to be taken into Christ's new humanity solely by virtue of the Son's assumption and subsequent vindication of human nature there are three important corollaries. Firstly, we undermine the inherent personal dynamic of sin. Sin is not an abstract, spiritual commodity removed impersonally by Christ. Rather, it is an inadequate mode of being, an offensive form of relating rooted in the dark and conscious veering of a will out of relation with its Creator God. Secondly, we remove the inherent contradiction of sin: the tension between sin as 'already there' and human freedom and responsibility of action. Thirdly, and of crucial importance for the doctrines of God and Christ, we confuse the distinction between the human person and human nature. Any vindication of the latter at the expense of the former undermines the tradition of affirming we are both responsible for our own (actual) sin as well as the mode of being (original sin) into which we are all born. Only a christology that meets with and resolves both characteristics of the tensive symbolism of sin can be deemed relevant to the human predicament. Any other is, for Irving, a characterless and impersonal form of religion.

[138]    CW5, 214.
[139]    CHF, 4.
[140]    CHF, 5.
[141]    R Frost, 'Desert Places', *The Poetry of Robert Frost*, London: Jonathan Cape, 1976, 296.
[142]    W Shakespeare, *Titus Andronicus*, Act 3, scene 2.
[143]    CW5, 43.
[144]    CW5, 107.
[145]    OCD, 133.
[146]    CW5, 80–86.
[147]    PW2, 165.
[148]    PW2, 165.
[149]    PW2, 164–165.
[150]    Archimandrite Sophrony, *The Monk of Mount Athos*, London: Mowbrays, 1973, 22.
[151]    CW5, 567.

[152] OCD, 89.
[153] OCD, 132.
[154] CW5, 322.
[155] CW5, 52.
[156] See CE Gunton, *Christ and Creation*, Paternoster: Carlisle, 1992.
[157] CW5, 116.
[158] CW5, 84.
[159] MW5, 393.
[160] CW5, 324.
[161] CW5, 86, 90.
[162] CW5: 84–86.

# Part III

Part III

# Irving's Doctrine of Christ

## Introduction

> As one man's trespass led to condemnation for all men, so one
> man's act of righteousness leads to acquittal and life for all men.
> For as by one man's disobedience many were made sinners, so
> by one man's obedience many will be made righteous.
> (Romans 5:18–19).

Central to any proclamation of the Christian gospel is the
belief that through the person and work of Christ the
capacity for human waywardness and rebellion against its
Creator has not only been arrested but has also been
replaced by a capacity for obedience. God, in Christ, has
reconciled a fallen world unto himself: the dynamics of such
a reconciliation being rightly understood, by and large,
within a theology dominated by the passion, crucifixion,
death, burial and resurrection of Jesus Christ. Without the
crucified and risen Christ we can do nothing. This is the
framework within which the historic church has sought to
understand its faith: the centrality of the cross. However,
this stress has, at times, focused on the work of Christ at the
expense of the being or person of Christ. Indeed, it would be
true to say that the former has often presented Christ in
isolation from the Father and, more so, the Spirit. Thus, the
great christological debates of the past have often presented
Christ in a manner that precluded any meaningful place for
both the Spirit and, consequently, our understanding of the
Spirit.
There are three possible responses to such an accusation.
The first can be mentioned and dismissed rather quickly,

125

namely, that this is a wrong interpretation of the development of Christian doctrine and therefore not worth pursuing. In the second response the criticism is deemed correct and therefore a proper application would be to dismiss early Christian thinking as irrelevant to our purposes today. In the third response to such an analysis, it acts as a stimulus for creative exploration in order to expand and develop the tradition we have inherited but perceived to be deficient in given areas, in the hope that by so doing we add to the deposit of faith delivered to the church. It is in this third way that we respond here as we turn to Irving's christology, for he himself seeks to bring out what is already there within the tradition he has inherited. It should come as no surprise by this stage in our discussion to discover that the manner by which Irving unpacks the person and work of Christ is intimately related to the less developed doctrine of the Spirit.

Parts I and II have outlined where Irving locates the person of the Spirit in relation to both divine and human being. In his appreciation of the person and work of the Spirit, Irving attempts to incorporate a more dynamic understanding of the Spirit. In so doing his christology becomes relevant in the manner by which we may understand better the being of God as Trinity, the person and work of Jesus Christ as Saviour and Lord, and the dynamics of spiritual life to which human being is called in light of the incarnation. In addition, such a method provides a foundation for presenting more clearly an understanding of the relevance of Christ. In Part III we can see how Irving unites the two in his christology, wherein the being of God and human being meet in intimate and personal union in incarnation. Therefore Irving's christology is the explicit concern here. In particular, we shall see that his understanding of the humanity of Christ, in its relation both to the divine and the human, is that we become more true to ourselves as we move towards Christ. Merton's sentiment regarding the nature of human dignity is particularly apt at the point,

> Souls are like athletes, that need opponents worthy of them, if they are to be tried and extended and pushed to the full of their powers, and rewarded according to their capacity.[1]

As we have seen, Irving's anthropology is motivated by his belief that human being is in its becoming, and becomes so only in so far as it stands against, battles with and seeks to overcome all that stands in its path to that goal. It is this, surely, that characterizes any relevant spirituality: a resolute stand against all that would destroy the human soul and spirit, the conscious, rational and wilful centre of human existence.

Yet why is it that when we turn to many presentations of Christ, one baptized by John, anointed by God with the Holy Spirit and power, who went about doing good and healing all that were oppressed, because God was with him (Acts10:36–39), we confront a sphinx-like figure, who although considered *totus homo*, complete man, was left devoid of the barest elements considered necessary to human spirituality? The citation of Tertullian at the beginning of Part II perhaps hints at the problem for, to a greater degree than the tradition that followed him, Tertullian understood deeply the relevance of Christ's humanity as being identical to that possessed by all in need of salvation. Consequently he is one whose spiritual formation developed in similar fashion to his fellow human beings. It is not insignificant that such an insight emerges from a Montanist background with its openness to the work and person of the Spirit.

The trouble is that the place of the Spirit in the life of Christ is more or less missing from the most important creeds which were to have such profound influence upon subsequent thought. This is not to presume that the whole question of the Saviour's humanity and his spiritual growth was not a topic of discussion. Only the most uninformed commentator on Christian doctrine could suggest that the humanity of the Saviour was an undiscussed issue in patristic theology. It was the very focus of attention of the most important battles with Arius and Apollinarius. However, what is lacking is a parallel interest in the relationship of the Spirit to the one proclaimed very God and very man. The how and wherefore of human development as portrayed, for instance, in the Lucan depiction of Jesus as the one who 'increased in wisdom and in stature, and in favour with God and man', came to be overlooked (Luke 2:52). After all, if it is through the Spirit that human obedience which leads to righteousness is attained, what does it say about our understanding of Jesus Christ if we deny him this dimension of life in the Spirit? Surely we must make sense of the 'master-image'[2] or 'master-truth'[3] of the incarnation in a way that embraces and makes sense of the Spirit?

The task, then, of systematic theology is to expand our 'epistemic priorities'[4] beyond the purely incarnational and incorporate the inspirational and show how the two relate. If the task of systematic theology is the 'attempt to state as correctly and straightforwardly as possible a theological perspective',[5] then the task for Part III is to do just this in relation to the manner by which Irving establishes a christology which makes sense of both the notion of the incarnation and the relationship of the Word made flesh to the Spirit of God. In order to do this, the theologian must not only be analytical but also constructive, able to go beyond the inadequacies and take up the challenge to advance new ways of thinking and speaking about God. The task in Part III, then, involves showing how Irving does just this in relation to his pneumatic understanding of incarnation. For if the gospel is about the reality of the incarnation, then it must enter the 'logical space'[6] created by such a belief. It must go beyond the act of enfleshment to the grounds and means by which such an act both comes to be and is relevant to the human need of salvation. Such belief allows us to create a logical space between what we may call incarnational and inspirational christologies, namely, the difference in method between that which stresses the Son and the Spirit respectively.

Irving prepares the ground by outlining the two poles which set the boundaries of this 'space'. They are the being of God as Trinity and human being in its becoming. My approach rests on two assumptions: firstly, that these are the central concerns of his thesis, and, secondly, they allow us to unpack his own understanding of the place of the Spirit in the incarnation.

The task, then, is one which needs to recognize both the particular and progressive in christological interpretation. It is particular in that the context within which questions are realised, problems confronted and solutions proffered, creates a change in the way we perceive the dynamics of the incarnation. It is progressive in that the ensuing perceptual shift itself creates a new means of interpretation, a paradigm, by which subsequent interpretation may be developed.[7]

Irving's christology may help us in such a task. In the same way that his doctrines of God and human being appear to draw from different traditions, so his christology appears to unite several disparate facets. He achieves this by making space for the Spirit in the incarnation in a way which does not pit the incarnational against the inspirational, Christ against the Spirit. It is almost as though he understands them to be different answers to different questions[8] which he now deems appropriate to unite, in response to the particular question facing himself. Rather than pit incarnational against inspirational, above against below[9], Irving offers a possible *via medians* through them. To follow this is to enter the 'logical space' about which we have been talking.

Whether consciously or unconsciously, Irving has adopted his method in order to assure both the Saviour's divinity and the believer's salvation. He appears to operate on three levels: the theological, anthropological and the christological. Whilst it would be wrong to suggest that each may be considered independently of the others, it is helpful to highlight each on its own.

Therefore, whilst Irving's entire thrust is christological, his doctrine of Christ is built upon an understanding of God and man. Between the two he constructs his christology. In addition, he holds them together with his concern for a true and viable doctrine of salvation. It is only in light of the human condition and its subsequent solution from within the community of sinners, that the Christian proclamation of good news makes sense. It is those who are sick who need a doctor, not the well, for Christ 'came not to call the righteous, but sinners' (Matthew 9:12–13). Now, this is hardly a novel insight into Christian doctrine: it stands at the very heart of the gospel and determines the entire order of salvation. So too for Irving. Most of the attention in previous commentaries on Irving has focused upon his doctrine of Christ and the debate caused by what he said about the humanity of the Saviour. Consequently, little, if anything has been said about how the doctrines of God and man are related in Irving's thought.[10]

Parts I and II have sought to outline Irving's doctrine of God and man as relatively self-contained units, gleaned from his sermons and publications, in order to present more fully, for the first time, each doctrine as it stands on its own. From this survey, Irving emerges as a theologian who maintains both the axioms he has inherited, and yet does so without repeating them uncritically. While he may be renowned for his particular doctrine of Christ and to those familiar with only the Irving-caricature, his peculiar doctrine, the previous discussion shows this christological particularity to be equally characteristic of his doctrines of God and human being.

Irving's doctrine of the Trinity, then, may be understood as a reorientation of the data already there. It is a re-presentation of correct doctrine—a making sense again of what was to become increasingly a doctrine viewed as a secondary, albeit important, expression of Christian belief.

The method undertaken in the previous chapters is not altogether foreign to the method employed by Irving. Although he did preach a series of sermons on the doctrine of God, neither in these sermons nor in subsequent publications do we find a systematic theological presentation. Rather, we confront the thinking of one who allows the issues at hand to interact with the tradition he inherited, in order to arrive at a more adequate understanding of the Christ-event. In doing so, Irving's theology underwent a distinct reorientation, but one that is not so much a movement away from the tradition, as an attempt to develop the data and concepts already contained within that tradition. What is so interesting about Irving is the way he unites the historical Jesus with the Judaeo-Christian God by means of both the incarnational and the inspirational, the Son and the Spirit.

Of interest here is the manner in which Irving understands salvation as a trinitarian event. In identifying this trinitarian understanding of incarnation the question to ask is whether this expression of divine being as Father, Son and Spirit relates solely to the human need of salvation, that is, whether it is economic relating to the economy of salvation, or whether it is essential, expressing the very nature of divine Being itself. For Irving, it is the latter, a significant fact when we consider that at the same time his immediate German contemporary, Friedrich Schleiermacher, was developing an economic interpretation of Divine being.

## A Contemporary Solution

In one sense a superficial comparison with Schleiermacher could possibly suggest that Irving was significantly out of step with contemporary theology. This, however, is very much not the case. His own attempt to unite his christology with the doctrine of God as Trinity was unusual for the time. Although the doctrine of the Trinity was part of the Christian story, there was an increasing uneasiness as a result of the Enlightenment thinkers regarding it as an 'addition' albeit a necessary one, to Christian faith. As we noted in Part I, by Irving's time this doctrine was seriously undermined.

Not surprisingly, then, that the doctrine of Christ underwent serious revision, for the Enlightenment, according to McGrath, raised three major christological problems. Firstly, the 'two-natures' doctrine of the ancient church was questioned as absurd and illogical. Secondly, it became increasingly difficult to maintain the uniqueness of Jesus Christ without recourse to the supernatural. Lastly, as the historical reliability of the gospel records were more and more questioned, there was an increasing skepticism concerning knowledge of the historical Jesus.[11] Add to this the inherent problems with the use of 'person' to describe each of the members of the Trinity, at a time when 'person' was widely understood to be 'individual', and it was not surprising that the idea of three persons yet one God tottered close to the edge of incoherence. The language of the creeds had become the Babel of the Enlightenment. Consequently, there arose, in light of such a critical shift in thought, the need to make new sense of both the God of Jesus Christ and Jesus Christ himself. The result was a critical rejection of tradition. The problem facing Schleiermacher and his seriously minded theological contemporaries was that of explaining 'how the trans-mundane, transhistorical monarchia of God' could be 'united with the historical economy of redemption, and in particular, its self-disclosure in Incarnation'.[12] Schleiermacher was to head a school of theology that has lasted well into the late twentieth century, one which clearly sought to re-educate Christian thinkers concerning the relationship between Christ and God. As Schleiermacher himself puts it:

> It is important to make the point that the main pivots of ecclesiastical doctrine—the being of God in Christ and in the Christian Church—are independent of the doctrine of the Trinity.[13]

Yet this is not to deny any sense of irrelevance: Schleiermacher is unequivocal about its importance:

> We rightly regard the doctrine of the Trinity . . . as the coping-stone of Christian doctrine.[14]

It is this recognition of the importance of understanding God in terms of Trinity on which Irving and Schleiermacher touch. For Schleiermacher the doctrine of God acts as an interpretative key by which we make sense of what God has done in Jesus Christ. Indeed, it is an open-ended key.

> We have the less reason to regard this doctrine as finally settled since it did not receive any fresh treatment when the Evangelical (Protestant) Church was set up; and so there must still be in store for it a transformation which will go back to its very beginnings.[15]

It is this sense of transformation that Irving surprisingly takes up, yet does so in a way very different from his contemporaries. Schleiermacher moved away from any understanding of God and Christ which eternally united the two in the way understood in the Nicene Creed. He was ultimately to perceive the relation between the two as merely related to the economy of salvation, in a way rather similar to that presented in the fourth century by Sabellius who considered that the 'Trinity was not essential to God-head in itself considered, but only in reference to created beings and on their account'.[16] For Schleiermacher, then, the Son did not exist before the Incarnation. There is no eternal Father, Son and Spirit: God is only so in relation to creation. For Schleiermacher, 'the whole Trinity is God revealed; but the divine Being as he is in and of himself and in his simple unity, is God concealed or unrevealed'.[17]

Alongside this reassessment of the doctrine of the Trinity was Schleiermacher's attempt to present Christ as the perfect man. He identifies two extremes to avoid:

> On the one hand one must conceive something in Christ that specifically distinguishes him from other men, and on the other hand holds fast to the view of really human conditions of life. One cannot say that these two tasks would really be carried out in mutual agreement in the course of the usual method of treatment . . . The truth of the matter is that those who hold fast to . . . dogma . . . fall into a docetism which holds that Christ in his true life is no true man, and all artificial aids that have been employed do not achieve what they were intended to achieve. On the other hand . . . those who take their departure from the attempt to represent the life of Christ completely as a genuinely human life usually end up by conceiving Christ in such a way that no intelligible reason remains for making him in any way such an object of faith, a central point of the world . . . and this is the division that characterizes contemporary theology.[18]

It is interesting to note that Schleiermacher, like Irving, overcomes such problems by turning to his understanding of Adam, the first creation. He is 'an imperfect state of human nature'.[19] But the second Adam, Christ, is not so. He is perfect: God is the highest operating principle in his life and in so doing, the human creature reaches completion. The latent and inadequately realized in human being is actualized in Jesus Christ. He is the true human being. But notice that for Schleiermacher it is an operation of God, rather than of the Son and the Spirit.

We return, then, to the very issues Irving sought to combat, as we have seen in Part I, and face the theological uncertainty Irving sought to redress. If God remains concealed we are in darkness concerning his true identity. If Christ does not struggle with our very nature as human beings we have no assurance of being able to overcome ourselves. Both Irving and Schleiermacher tackle the same issue: of making Jesus Christ relevant. It is noteworthy that whilst one, Schleiermacher, interpreted the trinitarian being of God in purely economic terms, the other, Irving, sought to give meaning to the person and work of Christ in such a way as to show God to be truly and eternally Trinity. Both sought to bring fresh meaning to the significance of Jesus Christ by means of a massive shift in interpretation. However, it may be argued that the Enlightenment project has failed,[20] and the Christian accomodations to Greek thought that went along with it. Its metaphysic does not allow, in the end, sufficient space between the doctrines of God and Christ. It is the contention of this chapter that Irving's perception of the incarnation, in which he gives place to the person and work of the Spirit in the incarnation of the Son and in obedience to the Father, provides such a space. Through expanding the place of the Spirit in incarnation, Irving is enabled to make sense of traditional language in its relation to the incarnation. By means of his essentially trinitarian interpretation of incarnation, and one in which greater meaning is accorded the Spirit, Irving is able to identify the place of the Son both *qua* God and *qua* man in such a way as to offer the believer, at the same time, assurance of salvation.

## Towards a Solution

Irving appears to be motivated in his christology on two levels. Firstly, that the incarnation reveals the glory of God.

Secondly, that the incarnation is seen to achieve its end: a saving action that meets the believer in his or her need. Thus, the incarnation can truly be said to be both an expression of God's justice and of his grace and glory.[21]

> The incarnation of the Eternal Word hath for its only beginning and origin the purpose of God to make known unto angels, and principalities, and men, the grace, and mercy, and love which there is in His own eternal essence.[22]

The sole purpose, then, of incarnation is 'to make known . . . the grace and mercy, forgiveness and love which (God) beareth towards those who love and honour the Son'.[23] Salvation cannot be separated from christology: the one who reveals is the one who saves. It is in incarnation that 'for once, mercy and truth did meet together, for once, right-eousness and peace did kiss each other'.[24] It comes as no surprise, then, that Irving's christology is determined by a strong concern for salvation. What constitutes interest in such a concern is the manner in which Irving uses the person and work of the Spirit to unite his christology and soteriology.

How can grace be given, the fallen be forgiven, the curse removed, sin stemmed, and divine wrath abated without any change in God's holy will?[25] He puts the dilemma thus:

> When . . . I perceived that . . . the church was coming into peril of believing that Christ had no temptation in the flesh to contend with and overcome, I felt it my duty in inter-calate in the volume on the Incarnation, a Sermon, (No III), shewing out the truth in a more exact and argumentative form, directed specially against the error that our Lord took human nature in its creation, and not in its fallen, estate. And another, (No IV) shewing the most grace and weighty conclusions flowing from the true doctrine, that he came in order to redeem us from the same.[26]

It is, then, important to turn our attention to Irving's doctrine of salvation. This involves us in looking at the relationship between incarnation and atonement. The two are intimately combined: atonement becomes effective only in and through incarnation.

> The question of the atonement . . . doth not so much grow out of, as it is involved in, and throughout implicated with, being of the very essence of, the incarnation; not a circumstance of its manifestation, but an original and substantial element in the idea itself.[27]

Only within the deep mystery of atonement does Irving ask his most profound questions. He is driven to explain the how and wherefore of his credo. How can the unholy creature be reconciled to the holiness of God without compromising that same holiness? At the very heart of the incarnation is the divine intention to reconcile, bringing about holiness in the human creature. God does this through the cross. Along with other theologians, Irving understands that 'without Easter Jesus' life would be a shipwreck that would reveal only the negative side of things—the limits of human possibility. In fact Jesus would be of so little importance that one could not take him seriously either as a question or as a model of shipwreck'.[28]

As we shall see, the context of the debate did not lie in the act of reconciliation itself, but in the means by which it actually worked. Such means are not reduced to a mere act on the cross: for Irving this would be too reductionist. It is sin that needs to be tackled, the sort of sin the human creature has to battle with daily. For this reason there is not such great stress on the cross as the unequivocal stress on the entire life and filial obedience of the Son to the Father as a life of sacrifice. The former can only be caricatured as a 'stock-exchange' theology and fails to meet the sinner in the daily cut and thrust with sin. It represents a doctrine of atonement that is more akin to primitive forms of commerce than to the divine response of love to a world that is bound by pain and trapped by its own limitations. Rather it is the entire act of the incarnation that meets the human need, not merely the bloody transaction of crucifixion. Only such a response on God's part meets the human need and vindicates the divine character: it is the historical application in time of an eternal relationship—of obedience and love.[29]

This goodwill of God to our race, this pity of God, this desire on his part, to see us righted, is the very basis of the work of redemption; which has no origin except in the love of God to man and man's world lost. If God hated man and man's world for their sin, and pitied them not, what did redemption spring from? As good cannot spring from hatred, but is the form of love, redemption is the greatest good, and therefore is the form of the greatest love. But redemption contemplates not a world in freedom of holiness, but a world in bondage to sin; and therefore there is no cause nor origin for redemption, save in the goodwill of God to a sinful race and a sinful world. Of this pre-existent love, of this unchangeable love, which there is in God's heart to His creatures, of this His special delight in man, and the habitual parts of the strong angelic herald is to my mind the strong demonstration; while, at the same time, it is the demonstration of the total inability of every creature but the Lamb which was slain, the Lion of the tribe of Judah, to do this mighty work.[30]

It is to the Spirit, however, that Irving turns in order to answer how this goodwill is worked out through the Son. For any christology to be ultimately meaningful it must make space for the Spirit. More modern commentators take this as a given: there can be no understanding of the Spirit without understanding of Christ.[31] Indeed, 'Christology must pre-suppose a pneumatology if it intends to do justice to the history of Jesus as witnessed to by the synoptic writers and if it is to preserve the historical tradition of primitive Christian christology'.[32]

The close association of the Holy Spirit with the person and achievement of Jesus Christ in his life, death and resurrection is the immediate foundation of all Christian understanding of the Spirit . . . Holy Spirit as Spirit of God is also Spirit of Christ, even Spirit of Jesus for the New Testament believers. The . . . spiritual and intellectual struggles which issued in the great conciliar definitions from Nicea to Chalcedon and beyond turned on the being, personal character, and salvific role of the Spirit. The historical eclipse of the Spirit in the theology and praxis of the Church may have been due to the exaggerations of a Christomonism as the historical emphasis on the Spirit may have seemed at times to obscure the specific nature and uniqueness of Jesus' achievement. Yet our whole Christian tradition insists on the indissoluble bond in divine origin and historical human activity between Jesus and the Spirit. Any understanding then of the relationship between the Holy Spirit and human identity must take account of the relationship between the Holy Spirit and Jesus' own identity as understood by the first disciples and the subsequent tradition.[33]

It is clear, then, that all christology should be founded on the life of Jesus Christ in his relationship with the Spirit of God. For Irving, a response worth engaging with must ultimately deliver the goods in relation to our common human need. It is a human need found not outside of the circle of salvation, but within, in the very humanity of the Saviour and the Spirit who upheld him.

## The Place of the Incarnation: That Which is Assumed

One of the major concerns which moulded Irving's theological development was the desire to overcome what Batson identifies as 'the divorce between category and experience',[34] of being able not only to communicate the message of salvation but also to ensure that it is seen to work. It is this pastoral concern that motivates Irving: a concern which drove him to focus on what Meyendorff describes as the 'crucial importance of (the) aspect of creatureliness . . . assumed by the Logos'.[35] Unfortunately, ideals are not always translated into reality, and the creatureliness of Christ has never had an easy passage throughout the history of Christian thinking. It is to this creaturely dimension of the incarnation, however, that attention is now turned, for it locates our attention in the very place of redemption, which can, in turn, be unpacked in terms of 'solidarity and power'.[36] In his solidarity with the human race, Christ identifies completely with a humanity in its being what it should not be. It is a solidarity with humanity in that requiring salvation: a situation or dimension more 'cosmic' than ethical: a bondage or 'power sphere' in which people exist and from which they require release; a realm of 'solidarity with the human race' which Ware insists requires 'not merely an exterior, juridical imputation of our guilt to Christ, but something far deeper and more costly: an inner, organic sharing . . . in all our brokenness'.[37]

For Irving, the efficacy of any given christology is the degree to which Christ shares in our brokenness and yet is able to initiate freedom from this power sphere. Implicit here is the notion that the divine Son is incarnated into *this* sphere, not another. It is a concern with what Gunton calls, 'the *ontology of matter*'.[38] Such a christology centres around the humanity of Jesus Christ as the Saviour of humankind, for, like Meyendorff, Irving correctly understands that 'the true dimension of the humanity of Jesus can be understood only in the context of soteriology'.[39] The history of Christian thought is to a greater or lesser degree agreed on this. Where there has been less concord is in the context of the creatureliness of incarnation, for inherent in Jewish and Christian anthropologies is the belief that human being has become that which it was not, and requires divine aid in becoming what it would be. The question, then, is whether the incarnation occured within the former, perfect state of humanity or in its fallen, corrupt state.

## The Humanity of Christ as Fallen Human Nature

The identity of the locus of incarnation is an important one, as it has implications for what we mean by redemption. For Irving, it is bound up with the identity of the Saviour's human nature. Sykes identifies four possible interpretations of the 'bald statement that the divine word took our flesh'. Firstly, that at the moment of assumption it was 'instantly transformed to be . . . a new type of humanity'. Secondly, that it was a flesh 'weakened by sin but not "naturally" tainted by it'. Thirdly, that it was 'sinful flesh, *natura vitiata*', and fourthly, that it was 'humanity as it was before the fall'.[40]

Irving is quite adamant in rejecting as a 'rather novel position' the position which believes that Christ,

> assumed human nature as it was found in Adam before he fell, as it was created by God ere ever sin was heard of—that he was

tempted no otherwise than Adam was tempted—that sin is but an accident of, and not essential to, our nature,—that Christ's body was not mortal nor corruptible—that he did not live by faith—that his holiness was inherent in his human nature,—in a word, that he was Adam over again, with the Son of God as the person informing and sustaining the Adamic nature.[41]

It is neither a pre-fallen humanity nor one sustained by the Son. Both tend towards two very distinct and well-refuted heresies: firstly, in relation to the humanity of Christ, there is the notion of Docetism, that is, the suggestion rather than the fact of a real human nature; secondly, in relation to the being of God, there is the suggestion that there were only two active participants in the incarnation, the Father and the Son.

Irving also refutes the idea of an instantly transformed and new human nature, the belief that,

his substance was the Virgin's, but that the Holy Ghost, in the generation, changed it into a new substance, by purging out all the impurities of the fallen flesh, and fixing it in a new state, wherein it should be liable to all our sinless infirmities, such as hunger, pain and capability of dying.[42]

This view lacks redemptive insight. The issue is much more to do with whether the one we identify as Creator and Saviour is able to condescend not only into the creature's realm, but to even that which has gone completely awry. Such an inquiry touches the very centre of the doctrines of God, man and redemption. Rather than locate salvation in what we are supposed to be, the true gospel both rises out of and reaches into where we have ended. The love of God not only transcends its own holiness but does so in order to reach us where we really are.

What has been overlooked by Irving's opponents is his intimate association between the place, agent and means of salvation. With this he develops a space within which to develop his own appreciation of the Spirit's role in incarnation and salvation. His entire christology is built upon the belief that 'the work to be accomplished must always be the measure of the power necessary to accomplish it'.[43] And this is achieved by an understanding of both the Son and the Spirit. For if the work of Christ in redemption is perceived only in terms of 'the bearing of so much inflicted wrath, vengeance, and punishment', then there will be little place for the work of the Spirit. Rather, it will be assumed that the divine nature itself is sufficient to bear 'the mighty load' and 'sustain the Sufferer'. Consequently, there would be little need for 'a third principle, and that a person, and a divine person also. Accordingly, the Holy Spirit in the work of Christ is almost or altogether avoided; which, however, is declared to have been the power in which He performed His mighty works, and offered His blameless sacrifice'.[44]

Rather, the crux of the matter is both the location and intention of salvation which Irving argues as 'manhood fallen, which He took up into His Divine person, in order to prove the grace and the might of the Godhead in redeeming it'.[45]

Here is where mercy and truth, righteousness and peace meet: in the union of divine intention with human need in incarnation. Whilst Irving himself identifies three possible types of human nature, that of the first Adam before he fell, that as it now is and has been since the fall, and that which will be in resurrection,[46] only within the second is the freedom of God revealed: to assume human being in the very lowest form of existence and redeem it. Indeed, there is only one possible means of doing so: for 'that Christ took our fallen nature is most manifest, because there was no other in existence to take'.[47] Indeed, Scripture would have said something on the subject had the Saviour's humanity been of a different nature from our own and immune to temptation and sin.[48] Only 'fallen human nature' suffices as the 'place of redemption'.[49] Irving outlines several implications of the belief that Christ's humanity is not in the same state as that requiring redirection: he is not tempted in all points as we are; he cannot be our high priest; he could only contend with two enemies—the devil and the world. We have no proof that he overcame 'the flesh'; humanity cannot be one with him since he was not one with it; there is no evidence that the Spirit has wrestled with 'wicked flesh' and overcome it; as Christ's life is 'no prototype' of the Spirit's power over sinful flesh, neither is his resurrection an assurance of our own resurrection to come; the gospels are a misrepresentation of Christ, for they show him to be as passive to temptation as we are.[50]

What, then, does Irving mean by the term, 'fallen human nature'? Although he does not expilicitly argue so, it is possible to understand his use of the term in two ways. Firstly, from an anthropological perspective, as that of solidarity. Woven throughout his thought is the notion of solidarity. Human being stems from the one source, the first Adam. It is a solidarity of nature, and therefore Irving understands humankind as participating collectively in the Adamic fall. As we shall see below, Irving maintains a clear distinction between human person and nature[51] and this enables him to assert that once we are overtaken by sin, we are not only in a state common to all humankind, but also in that into which the Son must come if the gospel is to offer an effective solution. Whilst 'there is a kind of necessity to use the term flesh'[52] when we talk in terms of incarnation, Irving wants to spell out just what this means for the deliverer and recipients of salvation.

Irving's understanding of sin as the 'state of a creature —the second state of a creature . . . common to us all',[53] a 'simple, single, common power . . . diffused throughout, and present in, the substance of flesh of fallen human nature'[54] enables him to interpret the Westminster Confession's assertion that 'The Son took upon him man's nature, with *all* the essential properties and *common infirmities* thereof',[55] in terms of a 'fallen human nature'. The Son does so because he is incarnated into this organic mass.[56] Whilst Irving argues for participation in our humanity, he also accomodates the language of imputation only in so far as he has set the limits of meaning. Thus, when he does use the language of imputation in arguing that 'in the flesh of Christ, all the infirmities, sin and guilt, of all flesh was gathered into one',[57] the negative connotations are tempered by the positive act of Christ in taking to himself our very own nature under judgement. It is a freewill act of an already self-existing being who, out of love for the

Father's glory and redemption of the world, becomes the Lamb of God who takes away the sins of the world by participating in fallen human nature.[58]

In addition to this anthropological perspective, we can, secondly, understand his use of the term 'fallen human nature' from both an understanding of sin and the world. It is a solidarity in relation to an 'apocalyptic notion of an evil aeon in which humanity exists and which explains the enormity and power of sin'. It is because apocalyptic imagery represents 'a person or a personal aspect' as an 'aeonic force' therefore that Paul can represent 'flesh' as both a 'human mode of existence and as a cosmic, demonic force'.[59]

This is an important distinction, for it enables us to assess the biblical warrant for Irving's use of 'fallen human nature' for Christ as a means of establishing his solidarity with us. Humanity is held captive to a force greater than itself. Thomas Erskine of Linlathen, Irving's close compatriot, in a similar vein argues that, 'the devil took possession of the flesh, and it is only through the death of the flesh that the devil can be overcome—the voluntary death of the flesh. Simply through faith in the death of Christ for us. It is thus that we have life'.[60]

It is with this double sense of solidarity that Irving defines what he means by 'fallen human nature'. It is a solidarity with both the common stock and common oppressor of human nature. It is a life characterized by actual identification with human being in its fallenness: 'For thy power depends not upon members, nor upon men of strength; for thou art God of the lowly, helper of the insignificant, upholder of the weak, saviour of those without hope', (Judith 9:11). As such, Irving's christology stands well within a biblical stream, from the psalms of desolation and hope through to Christ himself. It is a christology of offence: we move away from superhuman notions of Christ towards the notion of lowly humility. It is the difference between the way in which the Christian God becomes victor and that of the victorious god of antiquity. Jesus Christ comes to us not in the guise of some Perseus who cuts the head off from Medusa with the golden sickle of Hermes and flees with his winged sandals, hidden by the dark helmet stolen from the Stygian Nymphs. Rather, Christ comes as one veiled in human limitation, as the one who embodies humility and obedience and ultimate death before being exalted. Thus, as Gunton points out, 'the heart of the offence is not the divinity of Jesus, but the fact that the divinity is given through and with this lowly, poor impotent man'. It is this which Christendom cannot face, for such a christology 'offends both the individual and the established order'.[61]

What we believe, then, about the person and work of Christ must be worked out within the solidarity of fallen humanity. It involves what we believe about God's response, which can be identified in three major concerns. Firstly, concerning sin, the divine opposition to sin alone makes sense of the seriousness of the human condition. However, imputation alone does not reveal this response. Rather, the guilt of sin and the divine 'abhorrence of the sinner' are demonstrated much more poignantly in the way in which the Son comes to us, 'in the likeness of sinful flesh . . . by making the Word flesh; by making Him consubstantial with the sinner'.[62] Secondly, the Son is Lord of both spirit and matter. The nature assumed in incarnation cannot have been angelic, for this would constitute him only Lord of spirit. To be deemed Lord of matter, it was necessary for him to partake of human nature which connects both the purely spiritual and material.[63] Thirdly, there is the notion of will: the will is under the bondage of nature. As he states:

> By punishing man in his nature, as it were, rather than in his will, it shewed that the will was under the stern bondage of the untractable nature; under the obstinate, perverse law of the flesh; and could not be recovered otherwise than by the smiting, judging, and destroying of that flesh, or natural man, which sin had made its stronghold; that there could be no peace between the power of that natural law, which had overpowered the spiritual will and divine purpose under which the creature was formed at first.[64]

In addition to such theological concerns, is Irving's pastoral concern about Christian salvation. He wants to get beyond what he calls a 'doctrine of debt and payment, of barter and exchange; of suffering, of clearing the account and setting things straight with God'.[65] It is much more about assurance: that what is attainable through Christ is possible because he has already overcome sin in the flesh and in so doing not only redeems a fallen creation back to God but brings about the means for all to attain holiness. It is no source of comfort to the penitent sinner to know that one who was unfallen upheld the law; for such a one is an unfallen creature and therefore unfamiliar with the struggles and mortality of those under the curse of the law.[66] As Irving rightly points out, the mystery of human being exists in being alone and being with, in being an individual and belonging to a community. The meaningfulness of our christology is undermined if the focus remains on only one of these foci, for,

> we are not unfallen creatures bearing another's sin; but we are fallen creatures, bearing our own . . . And by loading an unfallen man with ever so much sin of another, you do not make him a fallen man; and that he should bear it, and that he should keep the law without offence, is no proof to me that I shall be called to keep the same law'.[67]

In that Irving identifies the place of redemption in fallen humanity, he attempts to make sense of the suffering of Christ, who, though possessing a fallen nature, suffers whilst remaining sinless. The question is not whether he suffered, for 'Christ suffered for the sins of others'. Rather, it is, 'How can suffering for another reach an unfallen creature?'[68] Irving unites two distinct ideas in order to answer this question: that death comes to those who have not wilfully acted against God, namely infants, and, that suffering cannot be experienced by an unfallen creature. We may summarize his argument thus:

1. Sin is the deliberate act of the will.
2. Suffering and death are the possession of a fallen creature.
3. Human nature is proven fallen in that it suffers and dies.

4. No unfallen creature can suffer.
5. Remove this distinction and the difference between fallen and unfallen is removed.
6. Children die.
7. Children do not exercise their will.
8. Therefore there must be a distinction between will and nature.
9. Therefore it is possible to have a fallen nature, thus suffer and die, yet not disobediently exercise one's will.

We confront, again, the centrality of will. Death and suffering come by sin. But sin is the acting of a sinful will. Thus, suffering can only come to human beings in one way, the way of Adam, by a sinful act of the will. However, in an age of high infant mortality, and to one who knew at first hand the reality of such death, this hypothesis could not stand up to the facts. Irving was well aware that suffering and death come to those who have had little opportunity to act against their Maker. Yet suffering and death do come to such. Therefore, Irving allows this fact to speak for itself: the solidarity of humanity testifies to the fact that 'suffering can come to a fallen creature, without any sinful act of its own . . . and that death can come to a fallen creature without any sinful act of its own': the proof being seen in every child that dies.[69]

Suffering cannot come to one who is unfallen, for 'there is not such a thing in the records of being, as that an unfallen creature should suffer. The will must fall first by sinning, before suffering can be felt'.[70] Here we undoubtedly meet the most tortuous part of Irving's argument: he holds as unquestionable the premise that suffering and death cannot be experienced by an unfallen creature. It comes only by a deliberate choice of will. Even this, though, does not fully account for human fallenness, for it cannot apply to those incapable of wilful disobedience. Therefore, there must be a distinction between nature and will. Our universal solidarity with death is to be located in the fact that we all share the same fallen human nature as the first Adam. We are capable of death in that we come from this stock. We deserve to die in that we, individually, disobey God. For Irving, the fact that only fallen creatures can suffer and die, and that children die who have never wilfully sinned, means that there must be a distinction between nature and will.

What, then, may we identify as the place of redemption? It is through identification of the Son with fallen humanity. Christ must be 'as truly a fallen man, as He is truly God'.[71] We are back to the trinitarian nature of God as he directs his love to our condition:

> To make flesh was the great end, work, and accomplishment of the Incarnate God, and was brought about by the consenting and harmonious operation of Father, Son and Holy Ghost, according to their eternal and necessary relations and operations; the Father sending the Son; . . . the Son assuming flesh; . . . the Holy Ghost proceeding from the Father and the Son, to be its life and strength, and holiness, its resurrection and glory. To this flesh we have applied the word 'sinful,' or 'of sin,' in order to express the state *out of which God took it*; the words 'sinless and holy,' to express the state into which God brought it.[72]

The ultimate point behind incarnation, then, is to bring 'flesh' out of the state of sin into one of holiness. As Irving puts it, 'What he took to work upon was sinful, sinful flesh and blood: what he wrought it into was sinless'.[73] This, then, is what is involved in the final goal of Irving's christology: to present a Saviour who can offer certainty concerning salvation here and now. However, this is not the only criterion he deems necessary for an effective christology. We now turn our attention to the second of three criteria we must identify before we can assess whether or not Irving achieves a doctrine of Christ that carries such assurance.

### The Agent of Incarnation: The One Who Assumes

In what way is Jesus Christ significant for salvation, the very ground of its being and reality? Christian tradition has sought, by and large, to affirm that God is not in Christ in the same way as he is in ordinary men and women, or even in the saints. The significance of Jesus Christ is his very

person. This is '*the* christological problem'[74] which Irving
faces squarely and fully at a time when classical christology
was beginning to come under severe strain from its more
modern counter-responses, a crisis which McIntyre rightly
assesses as 'resolvable only by a radical reassessment of the
basic *shape* of the doctrine as expressed today'.[75]

It is a question about the 'Who' of incarnation, which
Bonhoeffer identified as the question about transcendence.
Since incarnational talk refers to the Son, the question 'How
are you possible?' is insufficient. Rather 'the question,
"Who?", expresses the strangeness of the one encountered,
and at the same time it is shown to be a question concerning
the very existence of the questioner'.[76] In other words,
Christ is understood not only as one who lived at a particular
point in space, time and history, but, in some way, his true
existence precedes the moment of incarnation. From one
perspective we may say that the 'ontological must precede
the functional',[77] that is, there is a hint of existence prior to
incarnation, which for Irving is best explained in a trinitarian
manner in terms of the eternal Son becoming the historical
human. Yet, from an another perspective, we must say that
the ontological and functional should be combined,[78] that
there is a 'both-and' aspect to the story of Jesus.

As we turn, then, to Irving's response to the 'Who' and
'How' of incarnation it will be helpful to keep this sense of
'both-and' in mind, for this is the means by which he gives
meaningful place to the relation between the Son and Spirit
in the story of incarnation. However, in order that we may
highlight the two more clearly, we shall turn to the 'Who' of
incarnation first.

Traditional christological responses within the Western
tradition have, by and large, identified the 'Who' in terms of
the Son alone. Little real consideration is given to the
trinitarian nature of God. However, for Irving, this is not
enough. Rather, the answer must refer both to the Son and
the Spirit. It is a concern with ontology, that is, with the
identity of the agent of incarnation. It is a concern for the
identity of the one who saves. In this case, it is a concern for
the full trinitarian sense of agency in order to show how the
divine and human truly meet in saving action in Jesus Christ.

The clear distinction Irving makes between divine and human being, serves as the foil by which he identifies the dynamic of salvation as trinitarian rather than merely christ-ological. In some way he must show that in the act of incarnation the Son both reveals the Father's love and upholds perfectly his fallen humanity.

## The One Who Assumes From Above

> The person acting and suffering is the eternal and unchangeable Second peson of the Godhead. He is the *I* who was in the bosom of the Father from all eternity; and in every action He is conscious God. When He saith, 'I will,' it is the Godhead that willeth. From the infinite Godhead, therefore, is the origin of every volition and action of Christ. The fountain is there in the infinite.[79]

Irving's response is an unequivocal reiteration of ancient formulae which declare Christ to be one person in two natures. As he puts it elsewhere: 'The only person in Christ is the person of the Son of God; whose identity doth not change by his becoming man'.[80] Irving does not waver on this point. Without it there can be no revelation of the Father, for only God is capable of revealing God. Yet he does so not as an individual but in a fully trinitarian manner. Thus Irving argues:

> He was the person of the Eternal Son, manifesting forth the will of the Father and the work of the Holy Ghost, as well as the Word of the Son, in manhood, yea, in fallen manhood. He took up the creature in its lowest estate in order to justify God therein, by proving how good even that estate was.[81]

## The One Who Assumes From Below

Pursuing a firmly traditional christology, Irving is adamant about one thing: the agent of incarnation is not a mere human person. Why? Firstly, for the theological reason given above: if God alone saves, then God alone must be the author of salvation; human being, alone, is unable to attain such a goal. Secondly, on soteriological grounds, Irving identifies not only our natural human solidarity but also our personal. He distinguishes between original guilt, in which the Saviour participates, and original sin, in which only human persons participate. Thus, whilst each person experiences the unity of original sin and guilt, for original sin and the act of sinning are inseparable, in the Saviour there is only the taint of original guilt, as we have noted above. Thus, the Son is 'acquitted from all charge of original sin, by the fact of his not having been created' for,

> as Christ was man, and not *a* man, he cannot be spoken of as a human person, without being brought in guilty of original sin. As a divine person he is clear of it, and no one can impute it to him. His not having natural generation, clears him of it altogether.[82]

The question to be asked here is whether Irving is guilty of the ancient heresy of Apollinarius, for in denying that the Son assumes a human person, does he not deny something essential to being human? We shall address this later in our discussion, but before we can do so we must first assess Irving's intention in making such a statement.

Firstly, Irving appears to use 'person' as a theological tool with a very specific function: its meaning is to be found in Irving's doctrine of salvation. Only God can be both author and agent of human salvation. Secondly, he holds together two ancient and usually disparate christological methods by means of the place he gives to the Spirit in relation to the humanity of Christ. His insistence that there is no human person involved in incarnation should be understood in terms of the more ancient and ontological use of 'person' in what we may call 'Logos-flesh' christologies. In denying human personhood to Christ, it is not Irving's wish to undermine the humanity of Christ. It is, rather, an anhypostatic interpretation of the humanity of Christ, that is, there is humanity only in so far as there is incarnation, personhood only in so far as there is the person of the Son. There is no independent human person.

Unless we appreciate Irving's concern here in relation to the question of agency, we shall misunderstand him. Theologically, the person of incarnation is the divine Son. About this Irving is empathic. However, when we turn to consider the salvific intention with which Irving is so concerned, we discover a double concern, wherein one dominates the other but not to its exclusion.

What does this mean? Simply, that as one who is steeped in the ancient tradition of the church, Irving primarily understands this question about the person of incarnation from a theological perspective: it is a question about being. Thus he gives an ontological answer: it is the divine Son. To this extent, he talks of one person and two natures. Here 'nature' is understood ontologically, as that which constitutes the Christ as a full human being. Thus, when the identity of the agent of incarnation is considered from within this ontological context, Irving clearly stresses the person of the divine Son. It is a stress on the divine agent of incarnation in the light of the human need for salvation which demands that priority be placed on the personhood of the Son, for it is *God* who saves.

However, when Irving considers the identity of the agent of incarnation from a soteriological perspective he appears to make a considerable shift in emphasis, but due to the fact that his main concern is with the place of the divine in incarnation, this second consideration is less obvious. However, it is only within this context that the Spirit's relation to Christ makes sense, for it is a context within which he wishes to stress the full humanity of the one who brings salvation.

It is because Irving combines the two different concerns outlined above that he makes a distinction between human nature and human person. It is true that his bold stress on the humanity of Christ in terms of 'fallen human nature' coupled with an even bolder insistence that there is no human person involved in incarnation serves possibly to damn Irving's christology as a form of Apollinarianism. This criticism, however, is founded upon a misrepresentation of his intention and serves only to confuse. Irving's intention is, on the whole, to safeguard the assurance of salvation. He does so by holding in tension two complementary christological perceptions, combining the place and means of incarnation.

The question is, then, whether he does so in such a way that the divine Son replaces the human person. From a theological perspective Irving parallels the early Christian responses: whatever it is that constitutes us as human beings, that too we find in Christ. 'Person' is understood in purely ontological terms. However, we cannot leave it at this. On the one hand we would be ignoring the complementary aspect of his theology, his concern for the nature and dynamics of salvation. On the other hand, it would also leave his christology open to the charge that it merely repeats an essentially inadequate, early christology.

When his attention turns to the question of salvation, the stress is on how Christ can be in solidarity with our need of salvation whilst at the same time free from the penalty of sin. We saw earlier how one can be 'sinless' (free from original sin and therefore actual sin) and yet be 'sinful' (being familiar with human guilt, the natural consequence upon human nature of the fall). We are then in a position to consider the question as to how the Saviour can be one with us in our fallenness whilst at the same time be free from the guilt of sin of that common stock. The agent of salvation is described thus:

> You have original sin taken away in Him by the manner of His conception. He is not, as it were, an individual of the sinful individuals; He is not a human person; He never had personal subsistence as mere man; He sees the whole mass and lump of fallen, sinful flesh; he submits Himself unto the Father to be made flesh; His Father sendeth the Holy Spirit to prepare a body.[83]

Irving, however, is not content to stop at this point. It does not suffice merely to infer the loss of the essence of sin from Christ. The mere removal of original sin is insufficient to establish Christ's sinlessness for it cannot offer any comfort to the believer. Like Schleiermacher, Irving understands the uniqueness of Christ to reside in the manner by which he inaugurates a new humanity. However, unlike Schleiermacher, he understands it to occur through the sanctifying presence of the Spirit. At this point, we are now able to focus more specifically on the means by which Irving establishes his argument.

# The Means of Incarnation

## The Act of Self-Limitation

Irving's christology stands in direct line of succession to those since Chalcedon which, in the words of Schoonenberg, have expressed 'the plenitude of Christ by attributing to him, divine nature and human nature'. Yet his is also one which attempts to combine the life of Christ 'on earth and his presence in heaven, the condition of the "servant" and his power, his self-emptying and his exaltation'.[84]

Only by identifying the 'Who' of incarnation is it then possible to delineate the 'How'. Irving's account is, as we have seen, based on a trinitarian foundation:

> Before the infinite Godhead in the Son could act in the finite form, whether before taking that form or after, He must act not of Himself only, but with the consent and concurrence of the other persons of the Trinity. And this is not a small matter, but is in fact that which determineth all the rest.[85]

Of importance here is the manner in which the Son's mode of incarnation is given in terms which make full use of the 'soteriological drama'[86] as found, for example, in the christological hymn of Philippians 2. For it is only in relation to the goal of salvation that any talk of the Son emptying himself or divesting himself of his divine prerogatives, makes sense.

How, then, does Irving set out to accomplish his aim? He refers to the pre-incarnate act of obedience on the part of the Son in order to become the Lamb slain before the foundation of the world. Of importance here is the notion of kenosis, which Irving interprets from two perspectives. Firstly, the act of self-limitation is to be interpreted from within the counsels of God himself which are revealed to us in the union between the Creator and Saviour. And secondly, the incarnation is not to be understood as God trying to get things right after an abortive start.

For Irving, the act of self-emptying, kenosis, is the highest act of divinity. The incarnation is a willing act of self-

154    *Christ and the Spirit*

limitation, not a necessary one. It is the self-limitation of the Son as he identifies with humanity in its need of redemption. Yet the act of redemption is also harmonious with the initial act of creation: both are to be associated with the Son, and because of this are not to be seen as opposed to each other in any ways. Rather, they complement each other.[87]

Thus, kenosis for Irving parallels more modern interpretations of Philippians 2:6, that, 'Jesus did not reckon that equality with God meant snatching on the contrary, he emptied himself', an interpretation which Moule points out as rightly rendering 'Godlikeness essentially as giving and spending oneself out'.[88] And if this is so, as Hanson comments, then Paul is making the point 'that divinity is supremely manifested in human self-giving in fact in the human self-giving of Christ'.[89] For Irving, this can be only in so far as it is the human self-giving of the incarnate Son for only a divine agent is able to be so selfless. As Richard points out, 'selflessness is not the absence of the self as subject, but the absence of the self as object of anxious preoccupation. The selfless self can let go'.[90] This is the scandal of the New Testament: the scandal of a God who comes to us not in power, but as one who as 'utterly humiliated man . . . is not a derogation from or even a modification of the glory of God, but precisely the fullest expression of that glory as love'.[91] Kenosis, then, is not to be understood in terms of divine impotence or redundancy on the part of the Son. Quite the contrary: it is an expression of willing obedience on the Son's part to bring about creation and redemption. As such it highlights the love of the Father in his capacity to follow human being into its own 'far country'[92] in solidarity with that which requires redirection to its proper position and relationship.

Irving, perhaps, best expresses this in his own words in this lengthy, but appropriate quotation:

> The Son . . . did before creation assume unto Himself that limited form of the Christ, in which the Father saw before time, and independent of time, before change, and independent of change. His work complete in that beauty and perfectness to which it shall yet attain. And in this all-containing form of

being, image of the invisible God, fulness of the Godhead, the Son did created and order creation to the end of his becoming flesh, did take flesh, did redeem it, did glorify it, and is now bringing all things to be under it . . . There are apparent changes, as His taking flesh; but this is not a real change of His being as the Christ of God; that is to say, he who taketh flesh, is the very same whom God set up before the world was, by whom God created the world, who spake by the prophets. No change did His spiritual being undergo, in these acts of creating the world, redeeming flesh and the world. His spiritual being is that fulness of Godhead, which was the device and the joy of Godhead, in the purpose, and in the enjoyment of before the light was created . . . The rest is but the acting of the Son, thus limiting Himself, unto the end of bringing that form of being which He had assumed into outwardness from the Godhead itself; that is, unto creation.[93]

With this use of kenosis Irving expands the idea of self-emptying in order to express the mode of incarnation. The Son lays aside the 'mantle of His uncreated and incommun-icable glory', takes on the 'veils of flesh', clothes 'Himself in the likeness of man'[94] by means of action on the part of both his divinity and humanity, the one by 'self-contraction' to the humanity, and the other 'by coming into harmony with the former through the mighty power of the Holy Ghost'.[95] He 'emptieth Himself out of His Divine nature, and passeth into the human nature' and in so doing becomes 'a very man with man's very limitations'.[96] When the focus is turned to this aspect of incarnation, we discover the trinitarian means by which the Son, as man, performs the Father's will. If we consider Irving's high stress on the full coinherence of Father, Son and Spirit in the event of the incarnation as an expression of the principle that the external operations of the Trinity are indivisible, it comes as no surprise that the act of kenosis involves the entire Godhead in different ways. The Son's self-limitation is never separated from the Spirit's enabling: as we saw in Part I, in his divine person the Son is at all times related to the Father through the Spirit. So, too, in his humanity, there is a pneumatic, Spirit dimension. Although this cannot be read directly from the pages of the New Testament accounts of the life of Jesus,[97] for Irving it remains foundational to a meaningful doctrine of salvation. Our appreciation of Christ as Saviour is intimately related to our understanding of him as the divine Son. By and large, Christian theologians have been agreed on this point. Less agreed has been their understanding of the Spirit's role in this dynamic. Is it to be located in terms of the divine, the human or both?

As we have seen above, Irving introduces an element of assurance on the grounds that the Son of God is incarnated into the realm of human fallenness. In the act of 'self-emptying and man-fulfilling' there is opened the possibility of understanding the full humanity of the Saviour, as one whose divinity is limited in order that the humanity supported by the Spirit, 'might endure the weight of the offended holiness and justice of God'. The divinity is restrained in order that the humanity may be sacrificed for sin upon the 'passive golden altar' of divinity.[98]

Irving's purpose, then, in stressing the notion of kenosis, centres around the belief that there is a twofold character to every act of Christ: he limits himself in his divine status in order that the human nature may perform the act through the power of the Spirit.

## The Place of Self-Limitation: The Soul of Christ

We are now able to identify how Irving understands the 'How' and the 'Who' of incarnation. It is his own response to how it is possible to speak of the presence of the divine given the integrity of the Son's human existence. As it is necessary to tune two different musical instruments in order to attain harmony in sound, so it is with the human and the divine. The question Irving sets himself to answer is thus: How shall human nature, in the fallen state, be brought into harmony with the acting of the holy Godhead? In that the human will has never acted in harmony with the divine, how can humanity 'respond, truly and justly, in all things' to the divine? Irving's answer is unequivocal. They are brought together as one, 'in the person of Christ, where we have them . . . brought together without any original sin'.[99] The immediate question from this is 'How?' Only in relation to this question do we begin to understand the place Irving gives to the Spirit in incarnation.

Like Schleiermacher, Irving had to forge a way past the Scylla of transcendence wherein the agent of salvation is too other-worldly to be of any earthly use, and the Charybdis of immanence wherein the agent of salvation is too entrenched in the trammels of human existence to be anything but the example of human shipwreck, and an unsuccessful one at that. Irving's solution is to identify the human soul of Christ as a theological means, with which he joins an inspirational dimension to his thoroughgoing incarnational christology.

*Verbum assumpsit corpus mediante anima*—the Word assumed the body by the intermediary of the soul. With this Irving stands in a historic line of interpretation in his stress on the soul of Christ as not only the place wherein Christ is the Saviour of mankind, but also the means by which he is one with us. This line of thinking is expounded by Origen in *First Principles* where he argues that a medium is required in order for the Son to acquire human flesh, for 'it was not possible for the nature of God to mingle with a body apart from some medium'. Origin identifies this to be the soul of Christ which acted as a 'medium between God and the flesh'.[100] However, unlike Irving, Origen insisted that although Christ had a human and rational soul, it had no 'susceptibility to or possibility of sin' by virtue of being perfectly united to the Logos in its preexistent state.[101] John of Damascus, too, holds similar sentiments:

> The Word of God, then, was united to flesh through the medium of mind which is intermediate between the purity of God and the grossness of flesh. For the mind holds sway over soul and body, but while the mind is the purist part of the soul God is that of the mind. And when it is allowed by that which is more excellent, the mind of Christ gives proof of its own authority, but it is under the dominion of and obedient to that which is more excellent, and does things which the divine will purposes.[102]

This interpretation of the union between soul and Logos, then, stands well in the mainstream of Christian thought.

With this use of the soul of Christ, theologians could talk about the incarnation, of Logos-soul-body, in such a way as 'not to appear so incongruous'.[103] Thus, whilst Arius and Apollinarius fought over the very presence of a soul in the humanity of the incarnate Son,[104] there was a sense of unanimity in patristic thought regarding both the presence and nature of the soul of Christ. Not so uniform was thought about the function of the soul. Augustine, for instance, in arguing that the greatness of divine power fitted to itself a rational soul, and through it a human body so as to change the whole man into something better,[105] suggests that the divinity of the Son changes the humanity. Ambrose of Milan represents an even more explicit rendering, arguing that since there is no imperfection in Christ, when the Son became incarnate, it was perfect flesh that he assumed. In order to do so he assumed a soul, 'a perfect, human, and rational soul'.[106] And Aquinas, whilst asserting that the soul is the *anima media . . . inter Deum et carnem*,[107] equally denies that 'the grace of the Holy Spirit is the mediating form in this personal union'.[108]

For Irving, the soul is the medium of disclosure and the locus of intention. By means of this 'theological tool'[109] we are confronted with the most intense progression in Irving's theological interpretation of the dynamics of incarnation: a progression that holds together both the divine agent and the soteriological goal of incarnation. It reveals both how the Son may become fully human and how redemption is not only effected but also affected.

> He was not merely filled with the Holy Ghost, but the Holy Ghost was the author of His bodily life, the quickener of that substance which He took from fallen humanity: or . . . the Holy Ghost uniting Himself forever to the human soul of Jesus, in virtue and in consequence of the Second Person of the Trinity having united Himself thereto, this threefold substance, the only-begotten Son, the human soul and the Holy Spirit—(or rather twofold, one of the parts being twofold in itself; for we may not mingle the divine nature with the human nature, nor may we mingle the personality of the Holy Ghost with the personality of the Son)—the Eternal Son, therefore, humbling Himself to the human soul, the human soul taken possession of

by the Holy Ghost, this spiritual substance (of two natures only, though of three parts) did animate and give life to the flesh of our Lord Jesus; which was flesh in the fallen state; . . . but the soul of Christ, thus anointed with the Holy Ghost, did ever resist and reject the suggestions of evil . . . Christ's soul was so held in possession by the Holy Ghost, and so supported by the Divine nature, as that it never assented unto an evil suggestion.[110]

Several important factors are woven together here, the most important being the place Irving attributes to the soul. It is the central location of incarnation. The Son unites himself to a human soul which is assumed, in turn, by the Spirit. This is, however, no mere inspiration: the Spirit may possess and anoint the soul of the incarnate Son, but it is the Son who, in his humanity, wields the Spirit. In so interpreting, Irving avoids the charge of ousting the filial agent of incarnation, as perhaps some modern interpretations do.[111] What is possessed is by the Son: what is empowered is by the Spirit. In this way the humanity is one that requires the Spirit's enabling, even when assumed by the Son. It has to be so both from the divine perspective where God's being as Father, Son and Spirit is such that the Son always relates to the Father's will through the Spirit, and from the human perspective where it is the Son's prerogative to obey and reveal the Father, but it is the Spirit's to sanctify. By means of both considerations Irving crosses the Rubicon that has so vitiated understanding of the Son's relation to the Spirit in previous generations. For instance, John Cassian rejected such talk on the grounds that if 'the Holy Ghost gave assistance to the Lord Jesus Christ' then not only is the Saviour made out to be 'feeble and powerless' but that the Spirit granted things to Christ 'which he was unable to procure for himself'.[112] This is the very point Irving wishes to settle: that both in his divine and human natures the Son is unable of himself to procure salvation. Such a claim stands in line with any trinitarian interpretation of incarnation. It is not the prerogative of the Son to procure salvation in and by himself. Rather, he is the one sent by the Father and empowered by the Spirit, both in his divine and human existence.

It should be clear by now that whilst Irving agrees that the human nature of the incarnate Son is totally fallen and that 'without a thorough communication, inhabitation and empowering of a Divine substance, it cannot again be brought up pure and holy', he also stands against any notion that 'the mere apprehension of it by the Son doth make it holy'. Or to put it more clearly,

> He is not sanctified, but the Sanctifier; for He is not sanctified by another, but Himself sanctified Himself, that we may be sanctified in the truth. How then does this take place? What does He mean by this? 'I, being the Father's Word, I give Myself, when become man, the Spirit; and Myself, become man, do I sanctify Him, that henceforth in Me, who am truth (for *Thy Word is truth*), all may be sanctified'.[113]

Such a belief serves only to undermine the place of the Spirit in incarnation and in relation to salvation. It results in the apotheosis of Christ's humanity and annuls the trinitarian action of God in salvation. For Irving only the Spirit sanctifies and empowers the manhood of Christ and in so doing, 'is the manifestation . . . of the Father and of the Son in His manhood'.[114] Here we detect hints of the Puritan, John Owen, in Irving's theology for Owen identified several actings of the Spirit upon Christ:[115]

1. The Spirit forms the body of Christ in the womb.
2. The Spirit sanctifies the human nature at conception.
3. The Spirit continues the work begun at conception:
   a. Christ exercised grace through a rational soul.
   b. Christ's human nature has simple nescience.
4. The Spirit anointed Christ with extraordinary gifts in order to exercise his office on earth:
   a. Visible anointing.
   b. Christ gave himself to the Spirit in his public ministry.
   c. Christ was full of the Spirit.
5. The Spirit brought about the miraculous works during Christ's ministry.

6. The Spirit guided, directed, comforted and supported Christ.
7. Christ offered himself up through the Eternal Spirit:
   a. He was sanctified to God to be a voluntary sacrifice.
   b. He performed this through the graces of the Spirit;
      (i) Love to mankind.
      (ii) Zeal for God's glory.
      (iii) Submission to the will of God.
      (iv) Faith and trust in God.
8. The Spirit preserved his body from corruption and decay in the tomb.
9. The Spirit reunited his soul and body at resurrection.
10. The Spirit glorified the human nature of Christ.
11. The work of the Spirit towards Christ shows:
    a. He is the Christ.
    b. We love him.
    c. We will seek to be conformed to him.

There can be little doubt that Irving was influenced by Owen, but it cannot be argued that his christology is a mere repetition of Owen's. One of the major differences between the two is the fact that Irving attempts to unite the trinitarian being of God with the incarnation in a manner missing from that of the more precise and scholarly Owen.

## Trinitarian Agency and the Soul of Christ

Our previous discussion on the agency of incarnation should have made clear that it is the Son who is the personal agent of incarnation. The dignity of the Christ-event rests solely upon this fact: it is the divine person of the Son as the God-man who is the agent of incarnation. In his divine nature, the Father's glory is communicated and revealed by the Son through the Spirit. In his human nature, the Father's plan of salvation is effected through the Son in the power of the Spirit. In his glorified nature, the Father's will is executed through the Son by the same Spirit who is now given to the church. If the Son is incapable of being in his own strength alone the sanctifying or empowering agent, then a 'logical space' has been opened within which the personal role of the

Spirit can be more fully delineated. Here Irving finds the means by which he may safeguard the trinitarian agency outlined above, whilst at the same time establish how the work of Christ can be known to be of worth. In this manner, he not only assigns a significant action to the Spirit but also does not detract from traditional orthodoxy, and rather, expands what lies at the heart of the Christian gospel.

The platform from which he extrapolates the dynamics of salvation is strongly incarnational.

> When the fulness of time was come, the Christ, or Second Adam, had at first a body prepared for Him from the woman's substance, and a reasonable soul given unto Him by the Creator . . . To which the Son of God, the eternal word, having joined Himself in consubstantial union, He became the Son of man and the Son of God, in 'two distinct natures and one person forever'.[116]

The incarnational gives rise to the inspirational. In so doing, the foundations remain secure. As Hebblethwaite notes, if we cease to think in incarnational terms, and opt for an inspirational christology, then we lose both the moral and personal force, as well as the religious force of belief. The former reminds us that the Son became incarnate for our salvation, and that God took responsibility upon himself for our salvation; the latter, that it is into the trinitarian life of God that we are caught up, by Spirit and sacrament.[117]

Irving uses the human soul as a theological tool to safeguard the integrity of God's trinitiarian work in redemption. It is the medium of such agency. With it Irving interweaves three distinctly different levels of thought. Firstly, the human soul is used in a general somatic or bodily sense, in relation to the Trinity, as the following quotation highlights.

> The three persons of the blessed Trinity are all concerned . . . in the work; but, as it is the office of the Holy Ghost . . . to carry into effect what the Father willeth, and the Son informs with word, he brings the Son out of the region of Godhead, into the limited region of a child in the womb of the Virgin. The Son, though willing to add to his estate of Godhead the estate of

manhood, cannot do this or any other thing but by the Holy Ghost; and the Father, willing to send his Son into this lowly estate, must do it by the Holy Ghost, otherwise the Holy Ghost's acting in the blessed Trinity were avoided . . . At the point where a work of the Godhead comes into manifestation, and . . . outwardness, the Holy Ghost is the actor; while it is in the purpose, it is with the Father; while is in in the word, it is in the Son; when it becomes act, it is with the Holy Ghost . . . Yet there are not three distinct separate stages of a divine work, but forms of expressing it, as it is the operation of three persons.[118]

This somatic language, secondly, takes on further detail when attention is turned to the means by which the incarnate Son makes the Trinity known.

Was it . . . that the incomprehensible Godhead of the Father was dwelling in the body of Jesus Christ, who said, He that hath seen me, hath seen the Father? No: the Holy Ghost dwelt in the body of Jesus Christ; and insomuch as the Holy Ghost proceedeth from the Father . . . is one substance with the Father, and speaketh and acteth only as He heareth the Father speak and seeth Him act, insomuch doth the Father dwell in the man Christ Jesus. But this is not the mystery of the Father's Godhead . . . The mystery of the Father's Godhead, which Christ came forth to manifest, is this, That in the Father who is the fountain of the Godhead, generating the Son, and through and with Him the Holy Ghost, is hid and contained that incommunicable and inexhaustible fulness . . . The Father . . . is not any manifestation of God, but God unmanifested; and therefore He is so often styled God . . . To the end that there might be an Infinite and Incomprehensible to be worshipped through the finite and comprehensible, it standeth under the person of the Father, in whom the infinite Godhead of the Son and the infinite person of the Holy Ghost is worshipped, as well as the infinite person of the Father; but all standing under the Person of the Father, because of the offices in the visible, which the Son and the Holy Ghost had undertaken, for bringing into effect the Christ constitution, or eternal purpose of God.[119]

Thirdly, the soul pertains to what may be identified as the sanctifying dimension of Irving's christology, and it is to this that our attention is now turned.

## Sanctifying Agency and the Soul of Christ

And if indeed there be
And all pervading Spirit, upon whom
Our dark foundations rest, could he design
That this magnificent effect of power,
The earth we tread, the sky that we behold
By day, and all the pomp which night reveals;
That these—and that superior mystery
Our vital frame, so fearfully devised,
And the dread soul within it—should exist
Only to be examined, pondered, searched,
Proved, vexed, and criticised?[120]

Wordsworth's sentiments echo well the entire thrust of Irving's christology. His doctrine of human being expounded above in Part II has revealed that the general end of creation finds fulfilment in the specific goal of human being which is actualized in and through the person and work of Christ. It is a human *becoming* in relation to its goal. But it is also a human *becoming* from that which *is*—fallen and in bondage to sin. Far from there being a second creation from nothing in order to achieve what the Creator first intended, one in which the Son assumes a new and untainted humanity, Irving argues that human being becomes from out of what is already there. It is in the recapitulation of what already exists that human being achieves its goal. As such, and in response to the question suggested by Wordsworth, there is indeed hope for creation. But unlike Wordsworth, who represents Spirit as the Romantic, pantheistic force under-girding creation, Irving presents us with an understanding of Spirit which transcends such an analysis: it is the Spirit of the one who fulfils the Law of God, and in so doing brings about a new humanity from out of what is now dead to sin and makes it alive to God. He does so by assuming a human soul.

Such is the importance Irving attributes to this belief that he identifies three consequences of teaching that Christ had no human soul. Firstly, the biblical portrayal of his human feeling and affections would be a mere fiction. Secondly, his sufferings could only be a 'phantasmagoria' rendering Christ unable to lift the fallen creature to the throne of grace.

Lastly, at his death on the cross and in the tomb, the divine nature would be separated from the human and as such there would be no assurance that the two natures could not separate again. There would be no assurance to the creature dependent upon such a union to suggest that the risen God-manhood could not be cast off like an unwanted garment. In response to such possibilities, Irving stresses that the Christ does indeed assume a soul and that he does so in the manner of every human being, at conception, and that it was sanctified by the Spirit from thence, 'so that He was in very deed a holy thing from the beginning of His creature being'.[121] Only with such assurance is there reason for believing that the work of Christ is reliable. Only if the Saviour has a soul and overcomes the bondage therein is there hope for those who trust him. If the root of our condition is in disobedience and consequently a will in bondage to sin, then the solution lies in the freedom of that will from the same bondage. What is of pivotal importance for Irving is not merely the belief that unless the Saviour has himself overcome that bondage then we have no assurance of freedom, but much more that the Saviour must overcome in the same way that we must, if there is to be any realistic assurance on our part. As we have seen, it is the Spirit who upholds the humanity possessed by the Son. It is the Spirit who upholds the human will against that which is the common oppressor of humankind, and through the risen and glorified God-man establishes a new dimension to human being.

## The Wills: Divine and Human

There is little doubt that Irving was influenced by his early mentor, the poet and philosopher, Samuel Taylor Coleridge. It was a strong but distilled influence, for Irving took nothing from Coleridge unless it would serve his own ends. It was to Coleridge that he gave a personal copy of *Sermons, Lectures and Occasional Lectures* on which Irving writes as a dedication, 'To my Sage, Counsellor and most honoured Friend Samuel Taylor Coleridge Esq'.[122] Coleridge's influence upon Irving appears to have been in shaping his understanding of the place of the will in relation to the divine. In particular, Coleridge placed priority on will within his doctrine of the Trinity. For him, it is will 'which supports Being'.[123] Will is 'causative of all reality and therefore *in origine* of its own reality'.[124] In addition, will is not an impersonal reality: for Coleridge it is the very seat of personality, in a manner rather similar to Irving who asserted that 'the personality standeth in the will'.[125] Indeed, the personality is 'necessarily contained in the idea of the perfect Will' and is 'an essential attribute of this Will'.[126] It is the will that is the 'supernatural in man and the principle of our personality . . . by which we are responsible agents'.[127]

Coleridge could hardly be described as pedestrian: he was generally more complex than simple in his thought. However, when we consider that Irving had a clear understanding of the gulf between divine and created beings, we can understand Coleridge in a similar manner. Only, the former approaches the subject from his own understanding of 'will'. For Coleridge, the Father was Absolute Will to the extent that there was a real, almost ontological, gulf between his and the creature's will. As such, there is need of a mediator, which Coleridge identifies as the Logos, who solves the clash between the absolute and individual, creaturely will. It is the Logos who is 'the everlasting middle term uniting the One God with created substance'.[128] We can see here a clear parallel between Irving and Coleridge: as we saw in Part I, Irving understands the Son's relationship with the Father and his work of salvation for us human being in terms of obedient will. However, left at this, the only point of originality is Coleridge's turn of phrase with regards to will. We do not, as yet, cross the Rubicon that distinguishes his response from any other that focuses solely on the Father and Son. What about the Spirit? Does Coleridge offer us a possible rejoinder?

It is perhaps here that we detect Coleridge's influence on Irving, for Coleridge argues that the very essence of human being resides in the will, 'and this will under a particular form'.[129] Herein, too, we perhaps meet a means of seeing the reason why Irving refuses to say that there was an autonomous and independent human personality present in the incarnation of the Son of God. It is Irving's consideration of the humanity of Christ in relation to his human will, that redresses the imbalance caused by too much stress on the divine role in incarnation.

In *Opus Maximum* Coleridge identifies the goal of human being in terms of the will that 'has to struggle upward into Free-Will' through 'freedom' that comes about when the will is 'One with the Will of God'.[130] This is Coleridge's response to mechanistic and passive interpretations of human existence.[131] Freedom, for Coleridge, is found in the 'centre of moral being which is received *in struggling against bonds that prevent it*'.[132] However, in reality this state of freedom is not the case, but rather exists in bondage to a 'nature under the mechanism of cause and effect'.[133] For Coleridge, true human dignity is found in the struggle of the will to become self-determined, to live under the law of perfect freedom. What we discover with Irving is an attempt to articulate how this may be by means of the Spirit.

Coleridge, then, identifies sin, in a manner similar to Irving: it is lack of self-determination, and therefore lack of imaging the one who, as Absolute Will, is himself a self-determining Being. Sin is the act of a spirit against Spirit, a will against Will and lies at the very essence of human bondage: it is a bondage of the will. Christ, by contrast, is the one whose will is in perfect relation to the Law of God, and therefore sinless.

There is an interesting difference between the two. As we have seen, Irving emphatically holds to the belief that the Son assumes a will in bondage and in solidarity with fallen humanity. Coleridge, on the other hand, and like the later Jung, would not allow that God could dwell in a sick soul. Indeed, Coleridge wrote in the personal copy of *Sermons, Lectures and Occasional Lectures* given to him by Irving that it is a 'startling assertion' to say 'that only by the constant Action of Omnipotence exerted by the H-Ghost was Christ himself able to fulfill the Law in the Flesh'.[134] This has partly to do with Coleridge's interpretation of original sin which he places in the will and understands to be a self-caused order rather than something inherited from without, as argued by Irving.[135] In this Irving reflects a more Puritan than

Coleridgean influence, for it is in his insistence that the Spirit is the one who operates directly on the humanity of Christ, that Irving concords with the order of salvation outlined by Owen.

From Coleridge, then, Irving derived a clear and intelligent ontology of will that enabled him, firstly, to talk of incarnation in terms of will, and secondly, to locate the Spirit's place in incarnation and redemption within the dynamics of will. From Coleridge, Irving was given an understanding of Spirit that enabled him to expound in an intelligent manner the person, place and meaning of the Spirit in incarnation. The Spirit is the one who communicates and effects Absolute Will, the Father's will, to the Word, the Son. The Spirit establishes and upholds the humanity of the Son, maintains his human will against sin and establishes a new humanity.

We are concerned here with the human will of Christ for three reasons. Firstly, Irving's theology of will emerges from within an incarnational context where the major concern is to show that the work of salvation can be trusted. Secondly, by observing his appeal to the human will of Christ we gain a clearer insight into how Irving understood the humanity of Christ. Lastly, the relation between the human and divine wills is the fulcrum upon which an adequate account of the trinitarian nature of incarnation rests.

Irving understood well that if we stress too much the role of the Son in incarnation, that of the Spirit is more difficult to state. It is perhaps here that we gain a sense of perspective regarding the historical position Irving holds, for whilst the modern debate about Christ has tended to subordinate the divine to the human, we find the opposite concern with Irving: his concern is to safeguard the divine in its relation to the human in incarnation. Nevertheless, he does not fall into the abyss of monothematicism where the human is lost to the divine. Nor does he fall prey to any notion of severe kenoticism where the divine is lost to the human. Rather, by positing the human will in its relation to the divine, Irving attempts to avoid both. He puts it this way:

He, the person of the Son of God, acting faith upon his Father through those temptations and limitations of sinful flesh, and receiving from the Father, the Holy Ghost, in answer to his prayer, did inform his human nature with such strength, light, life, and sanctity, as to overcome with its weakness and penury the utmost might of the devil.[136]

This element of faith on the part of the Christ is identified as seminal on Irving's part for two reasons. Firstly, although it does not appear explicitly at all points of his thinking, it holds an important place in his argument. Secondly, it is possible that in this area of thought he was also influenced by Thomas Erskine of Linlathen. Erskine, a fellow countryman, was himself influenced by Irving's notion of the fallen condition of the Saviour's humanity, and developed his own understanding about the place of faith in the life of Christ and the believer.[137] Nevertheless, whilst his insight into the place of faith in the life of Christ may be a latent development in his thought, it is far from one that is undeveloped, for, it must be stressed, it undergirds his entire understanding of the humanity of Christ.

If the Son in and of himself is unable to sanctify the fallen human nature into which he is incarnated, it is due to the fact that, on the one hand, he does not require sanctification in his divinity and, on the other hand, that it is not his personal function to sanctify. Rather, it is the human nature that is in need of sanctification, and hence of empowering by the Spirit. Sanctification clearly occurs within the realm of the human. Whilst the Father's will is accomplished by the Son through the Spirit, the dynamic by which this occurs is not brute divine power, but faith actualized by the God-man. In his humanity the Son exercises faith in the Father, and in so doing, receives the Spirit of holiness for sanctification. Thus, underlying Irving's entire christology, is a stress on the faith of Jesus Christ, as a human being upon the Father, in order to bring about the divine end.

Though the flesh, the devil, and the world, seek to bring the soul into captivity of sin, he through the soul, apprehending by faith the help of the holy Spirit, did resist the devil and the world, and the mortal corruptible flesh, and devote all the members of his body to the service of the living God.[138]

What is significant about this passage is the way in which we see why Irving combines this stress on the soul of Christ with an equally emphatic stress on the place of the will in incarnation, for he immediately goes on to argue that:

> the great combat is for the body, because the body is that which brings the soul to light. Man is made on very purpose to bring the invisible God to light, to be his image and his likeness, through which he may be seen and known in his working over the creation. Now God, being a Spirit, carrieth on his communication only through the Spirit or word, and not otherwise. There his operation as God beginneth and endeth. He leaves the will of man to do the rest. For he would have the will of man to be recognised as the lord of all visible things. By and through the will of man, he would use the body of man to express . . . what is the image and purpose of the divine mind, with respect to things created and made.[139]

A more modern commentator has put it,

> The very unity of the threefold God is as it were put at risk in the incarnation, in Jesus' total dependence on faith and prayer in his temptation.[140]

Human will is the place and means of redemption. It is the place in that it is from the will that human action, purpose, desire for knowledge and exertion of power originate. But it is a will which in its fallen state is in 'a condition of bondage, not willingly obedience', one from which it is unable 'to extricate itself into the obedience of God and the desire of everlasting good'.[141] It is the place of redemption in that in its fallen state it is 'loaded with a thousand oppressions, and not capable of being extricated but by the omnipotent will of the Father'.[142] It is the means by which redemption is procured because the will, as that which reflects the divine image, must be liberated from the power of sin in the flesh for it to reimage the divine.[143] For such reasons it is *this* humanity which Christ 'found all sullied and vile, and by His use of the Holy Ghost, did restore to its original excellence'.[144]

The question of Apollinarianism, that is, of something

inherently human in Christ being replaced in some way by something divine, in such a way that its humanity is endangered, was raised earlier. That Irving denies there to be any human person, is beyond question due to his desire to safeguard both the status and sinlessness of the Saviour. It is the consequence of a thoroughly incarnational christology. However, such a perspective is only part of Irving's christology, for alongside this stress on the divine is an equally strong insistence on the humanity of the Saviour, a humanity so completely in solidarity with that which needs to be saved that Irving identifies it as 'fallen human nature'. And as we saw with Coleridge, the notion of will serves very much to suggest that there was nothing lacking in the Saviour's humanity.

Perhaps here we touch on a semantic problem. It is clear that everything that makes us human is there in the Saviour. In the twentieth century we wish to talk of the person in psychological rather than ontological terms. As EL Mascall comments concerning the christologies of his day, a century later, they have conceded too much to the *Zeitgeist* of the day by transferring 'the whole Christological problem from the ontological to the psychological plane'. As Mascall observes,

> The classical Christian formula, 'Two natures, a divine and a human, united in one divine Person,' does not render the humanity of Christ incomplete, even while it implies that he has no human person, simply because 'person' is a purely ontological term and does not denote a psychological constituent of human nature.[145]

Irving and Coleridge were more concerned with ontology, but not in such a way as to suggested that there were two principles of determination in Christ, two 'persons'. By virtue of his understanding of the Spirit's place in incarnation Irving presents a Christ that is fully human. Before we consider how he unites both the inspirational and incarnational, perhaps Irving can have the last word on the relation between the divine and human wills in relation to Christ.

The orthodox doctrine is, that there were two wills in Christ; the one the absolute will of the Godhead, which went on working in its infinite circles, the other a man's will, which was bounded by the limited knowledge . . . desires . . . affections . . . actions of manhood; a Divine nature, and a human nature, God and man. The doctrine holdeth . . . that from the incarnation onwards, and for ever, Son of God never thought, felt, or acted, but by condescending out of the infinitude of the Divine will, into the finiteness of the human will; in which condescension, the self-sacrifice . . . humiliation . . . grace, and goodness of the Godhead are revealed: without which condescension these attributes of the Godhead could never have been known unto the creatures. This condescension it is which giveth an infinite value to every act of Christ,—in the Father's sight, inasmuch as it makes Him known, and obtains his great purpose of self-manifestation—in the creature's sight, inasmuch as it shews unto the creature the great freewill condescension of the Son, by which the Son is made known, and the Holy Spirit communicated.[146]

## The Son of Man: The Mediator

It is necessary to observe, that Christ, although not a human person, ever acteth as a human person, under the condition of a human person, within that defined sphere of creature being; and this is the meaning of His name, the Son of Man. But while thus acting within bounds, He ceaseth not to be the Son of God.[147]

Thus are we introduced to Irving's understanding of Christ as the Son of Man, an identity he carefully subordinates to that of Son of God, for the actings of the Son of God end where those of the Son of Man begin. It is the Son of Man who suffers and acts as one filled with the Spirit.[148] This important qualification hints at Irving's christological concern. The Son, as agent of incarnation, acts within the limitations of human personhood. Herein we are closest to an explicit outline of Christ's human identity. Yet it is an approach grounded firmly within an ontological setting. There is a sense of integrity in this method: Irving's concern is to establish assurance of salvation. Salvation, whilst effected within the realm of the human, comes about by the agency of the trinitarian God alone. It is hardly surprising, then, that Irving does not approach the question of identity regarding the one who saves, from a human perspective. It is not a man who saves. It is the Son of Man. Yet, it is as the person of Son of God that the 'personality of the Son of Man' is sustained.[149] It is the incarnate Son of God. As Irving puts it:

> The person, the *I* who speaketh, acteth, sufferth in Christ, is not the Divine nature, nor is it the human nature, alone; but it is the Divine nature having passed into the human nature, and therein effecting its will and purpose of acting or of suffering.
>
> By assuming into Himself the human nature, and becoming the Christ of God, the personality of the Son is still the same: it is the eternal, only-begotten Son of God, who speaketh . . . heareth . . . acteth . . . suffereth, and yet the Divine nature is ever distinct, and never to be confounded with the human nature . . . The words, and acts, and sufferings of Christ, are not to be called the Divine nature only, nor of the human nature only, but of the person, Christ, God-man; one person, through two natures.[150]

It was Kierkegaard who said that, 'man needs a mediator in order to come to God'[151] echoing the earlier Paul to Timothy, 'For there is one God, and there is one mediator between God and men, the man Christ Jesus'.[152] Nowhere do we meet the soteriological drama more clearly than at this point. For at the heart of the Christian gospel lies a dual affirmation. There is a gulf between Creator and creation due to the divine reaction to sin. The holiness of divine Being precludes his turning a blind eye to sin. The reality and offence of human disobedience and bondage must be confronted and overcome before reconciliation between the human and the divine can occur. For Irving, the divine response in the incarnation reveals the Trinity in the way that the Father's love responding to the Son involves the Spirit. At the same time there is the human plight, which is totally a bondage to sin. An adequate doctrine of salvation must not only take account of the divine response to sin and the sinner. It must also be seen to have dealt with the power sphere of sin. The humility, love and grace of God is revealed in the Son's willingness not only to become one with the human condition which requires release, but also to effect redemption in human rather than divine terms.

The divine and human, holy and unholy, infinite and finite, Creator and created meet in the Mediator. It is in the person of the one Mediator that Godhead and creature meet. Jesus Christ is 'the surety of a better testament' (Hebrews 7:22). As surety, Christ, in becoming our bondsman or bailsman,[153] is the divine assurance that God will 'fulfill his testament' and the human assurance that the debt has been paid. Both aspects are united in the Mediator who comes in the 'very condition' of the 'offended persons' and in the very condition of the 'offending persons'.[154] Christ carries out both the assurance that God will be faithful to his promises and the assurance that the debt is paid, not in his divine nature, but in his human nature, as Son of Man. Why? Because his divine nature is unchangeable and all insufficient. As Brunner points out, it is as Mediator that the Son makes himself 'one with humanity in its sin and sorrow'. In so doing, the incarnation is seen to be no 'mere gesture; it is reality, stark and painful. Jesus drinks the cup of human existence in all its alienation from God, to the very dregs'.[155] For Irving, however, the point must be made clear that the Son does so only in and through the power of the Spirit, for the status of Mediator and the effects of Mediatorship cannot be separated. To quote Brunner again, Christ's being as Mediator cannot be divorced from his work as Mediator, 'for this Person is not static but dynamic'.[156] Such a comment very helpfully serves to endorse Irving's intention in uniting the doctrine of God as Trinity so intimately with his doctrine of Christ.

We have noted already Irving's concern to establish the solidarity of the Saviour with that which is in need of forgiveness and restoration. This he finds in the humanity assumed in incarnation. We have noted also that, as a consequence, his christology does not stress the idea of imputation in his doctrine of salvation. Rather, it is one of identification. The Son identifies wholly and completely with us in terms of overcoming, rather than merely bearing an imputed punishment that still leaves us impotent against the ravages of sin. Yet it is an identification by means of dedication. Through the act of incarnation mediation is made possible. This is the theological framework within which Irving operates. Whatever we may wish to say about the place he attributes the Spirit his christology is essentially one of incarnation. His contribution is the way in which he appreciates the place of the Spirit in his relation to the incarnation. Although mediation between God and man is accomplished in the event of the incarnation, a mediation whereby the Mediator brings humanity and in particular, human will, out of the power sphere in which it finds itself enslaved and into holy obedience to the Father, it is by virtue of his doctrine of the Spirit that Irving gives his christology its distinctive shape.

## Summing Up

Thus we see how Irving safeguards the divine initiative in salvation: it is only God who can save, and therefore his stress on the Son's role. At the same time, he safeguards the human need in asserting that only that which is assumed, is healed. Both are part of the essential content of theology for incarnational christologies. What Irving adds to the traditional themes is the Spirit's relation to the Son, both in his eternal relation and in his saving role. Without the Spirit's role, there is no meaningful and assuring doctrine of salvation. For Irving, this entails the assurance of what he calls 'holiness in the flesh'—an assurance that what God requires of us is possible due to the fact that it has been achieved by the Saviour under the same conditions as those in which every human being exists.

By refusing to divorce the person from the work of Christ, Irving expanded the tradition he has inherited to incorporate a more fully trinitarian theology of Christ. It involves the full cooperation of the Spirit. In addition, Irving's doctrine of sin and his priority of wills in incarnation, gave an equal place to the role of the Spirit. Not only is the divine will expressed in the Son's obedience to the Father, through the Spirit, but also the human will is expressed in the mediation of the incarnate Son as Son of Man, through the power of the Spirit, upholding the human will within the limitations of human personhood and thus able to present it holy before the Father.

Accordingly, it could be argued that Irving presented his contemporaries with as stark an alternative as was possible to that which Schleiermacher was presenting across the Channel. Whilst the latter divorced completely the place of the Spirit from the life of Christ, the former battled to give the Spirit more significance than he had previously been given.

By means of the place he accords the Spirit in the incarnation of the Son, Irving avoids creating a tension between the person and work of the Mediator, of appropriating the being of the Mediator to the Son as God, and the work of the Mediator to the Son as man. To do that would be to miss the entire thrust of an adequately trinitarian understanding of the incarnation. Rather, the latter, the work, depends on the former, the person, in and through the empowering of the Spirit. As we saw in Part I, Irving's doctrine of God is thoroughly trinitarian, and according to it the Son performs the Father's will in and through his relation to the Spirit. In Part II Irving was seen to develop a doctrine of human being which clearly contained a spiritual dimension: human being becomes what its Creator intended only in and through our dependence upon and relation to the Spirit. Part II also highlights the manner by which salvation is attained: through the medium of fallen and rebellious humanity. Irving unites these separate issues through his understanding of the Mediator, the Son of Man. As Mediator, the Son continues to act in dependence upon the Spirit in order to bring about the Father's place of salvation, for 'in the days of his flesh, Jesus offered up prayers and supplications, with loud cries and tears, to him who was able to save him from death, and he was heard for his godly fear. Although he was a Son, he learned obedience through what he suffered; and being made perfect he became the source of eternal salvation to all who obey him, being designated by God a high priest after the order of Melchizedek' (Hebrews 5:7–10).

As Mediator, the Son brings together, in harmony and without default, both parties involved in the relationship at issue: a holy God and a rebellious creature. This is the Son's *nobile officium* in the act of incarnation. However, as Mediator, the Son depends upon the Spirit in order to restrain the rebel and fallen human will. This is the great comfort and assurance of salvation that Irving seeks to establish, for 'since we have a great high priest who has passed through the heavens, Jesus, the Son of God, we hold fast our confession. We have not a high priest who is unable to sympathize with our weaknesses, but one who in every respect has been tempted as we are, yet without sin. Therefore we draw near to the throne of grace with confidence, that we may receive mercy and find grace to help in time of need, (Hebrews 4:14–16).

As a result, Christ can become Mediator for that which requires mediation, in two ways. Firstly, in a general sense in that he assumes the general state of human being. As fallen human being he is one in solidarity with that which requires redemption. In his resurrection he is shown to be the prototype of a new humanity, and the guarantor of its final outcome, for in redemption we receive the Spirit of the one who himself has overcome both sin in the flesh and death. Alternatively, Christ is Mediator in the specific sense in that he assumes a specific human will which, within the limitations of fallen humanity, is seen to overcome the rebel nature and present itself unblemished to a holy God.

In this manner Irving safeguards the human subject of the incarnation. When he deals with that which is in need of salvation, as opposed to the one who saves, he stresses the full humanity of the Saviour, doing so within an ontological, as opposed to a more modern and psychological, interpretation of personhood. The agent of incarnation is the Son who, within the form of Mediator, as the Son of Man, limits himself generally in terms of fallen human nature. Specifically he limits himself in terms of his human will which overcomes the general state of incarnation, fallen humanity, through the enabling agency of the Spirit. It is a human limitation expressed in terms of will, in that the act of salvation has to do with the very essence of human being, of a will in bondage both to the law of fallen nature and to the spirit of the age.

Thus Irving attributes the general state of human nature in its fallen state to a power sphere in which all human beings find themselves enslaved. He does so in relation to the Saviour as Son of God. Additionally, he attributes the specific state of human being to a will in bondage to the present aeonic power, and does so as Son of Man, as Mediator. We can identify the Spirit's place in two ways here. Firstly, with regards to the person of the Spirit, any act of God the Father and Son always involves the Spirit. It is the triune God who mediates himself in the act of mediation. Secondly, with regards to the work of the Spirit within the economy of salvation, the work of the Spirit in relation to the Son who takes on fallen humanity, the Spirit empowers the Son to perform the Father's will and overcome 'sin in the flesh'. In so doing, the Son proves himself to be Saviour and Lord not in his brute divine power, but in humility. The human dimension is safeguarded in the act of assuming that which needs to be saved, rather than overriding it and annulling its very real power.

In his understanding of the Son's relation to the Mediator both as God and man, and of the Spirit's place in this filial role, Irving redressed the imbalance so prevalent in Western christology which stressed the divinity of the Son at the expense of his humanity. Such a stress undermined the identity of Jesus the man, the human representative, and rightly precipitated an alternative response which sought to establish the very human qualities lacking in the former conception. However, this reactive christology lost the space created and needed if Jesus Christ is to have any meaningful relation to the divine. Both, to greater and lesser degrees respectively, failed to make sense of either the Spirit's role in the process of salvation we have identified in terms of the incarnation, or the triune nature of the Christian God. Irving does say something provocative and challenging about the way in which he locates the Spirit. 'When we examine his writings . . . and when we allow for his rather extravagant style, we find a clarity of thought, a depth of understanding, and often powerful exposition and persuasive argument. Many of his points of exposition must carry our assent'.[157] Of particular importance is the way in which he brings content and meaning to the place of the Spirit's relation to the Son within the entire scope of incarnation.

> He took unto Himself a true body and a reasonable soul. He did not take these that they might lie beside Him unoccupied, or that they might be used now and then as it pleased Him . . . He is one person, the person of the Son of God, and every act of that person must include both natures, but never in either nature be perfected. If He did act in the Divine nature anything without the human nature, then there is a person standing in the Divine nature alone; for that which is distinctive of a person is a complete action, feeling or word. If, again, He did any act in the human nature alone, where is the divine? . . . God gave this revelation to Jesus Christ, who in becoming man truly came into limitation of the knowledge, feelings, and complete nature of man; self-contracted, self-humbled, self-emptied of His glory, that He might show His love to human nature in its lowest forms, and redeem it of its most miserable conditions . . . That human reason which he took, He did inform with His personality of the eternal Word; and receiving the Holy Ghost from the Father, in answer to His faith, He did instruct and support the human nature through all the stages of its existence, which was upholden wise, faithful, and true, through the influence of the Holy Ghost. And thus every action begun in the Godhead of the Son of man, proceeded into the manhood, and out of the manhood passed complete.[157]

## Conclusion

What, then, may we conclude about Irving's christology? There is no doubt about the truth of Strachan's statement that Irving's christological position appears 'to be unique and deserves the attention which it has so far not received'.[159] In our discussion of Irving's doctrines of God and human being, we have seen that the means by which Irving establishes the uniqueness of Christ are themselves far from ordinary expressions of his theological tradition. Rather, although they cannot be deemed totally unique, they do represent a significant development of elements within his theological tradition that have lain undeveloped and are themselves worthy of further attention. By virtue of such developments, Irving constructs a christology we may deem *efficient* in establishing a continuity between the object of the incarnation, namely, human being in its need of salvation, and the subject of the incarnation, namely, the God who saves. The person of Christ is at all times the central character. There is little original material here. However, when we turn to the place accorded to the Spirit we find that Irving reveals an original contribution in the way he unites the triune character of God with human being as it lives in relation to its Creator. It is by virtue of his doctrine of the Spirit that Irving establishes the theological continuity between all the agents of the soteriological drama. And in this we confront a sense of elusiveness, as Schweizer points out;

> If what we mean by Holy Spirit is that God is present and active on earth, then all Jesus' works are nothing else but the life of the Spirit of God. But the fact that Jesus does not speak *about* the Spirit but rather acts and speaks in the Spirit points to something crucial. In the work of the Spirit we once more encounter God in the first place as a stranger, the unexpected One, the One who cannot immediately be pinned down in an intelligible doctrine.[160]

The difficulty, then, is that the very attempt to articulate the Spirit into an intelligible doctrine is riddled with problems. If left in isolation, any doctrine of the Spirit tends to abstraction. However, Irving manages to earth the Spirit within wider theological and christological contexts. If it is true that any satisfactory doctrine of the Christian God depends on a satisfactory understanding of the person of Christ, then it is equally true, for Irving, that such a christology entails a satisfactory understanding of human being. For Irving, each of these considerations centres around the person of the Spirit. What is of interest with regards Irving's solution is that it involves the traditional teaching of God as Trinity and Christ's dual nature with a very vibrant doctrine of the Spirit. His contribution, therefore, serves as a bridge between that which he eschews and more modern Spirit christologies the responses of which start from the belief that 'our present official Christology, and doctrine of the Trinity which is built upon it, is not only expressed in the language of a philosophy which is outmoded and long since discredited, but also in one which no longer serves the interests of vital religion'.[161]

Whilst the blame for such a criticism lies squarely with the way in which our doctrines of God and Christ have been developed in what Ritschl calls a 'monthematic' manner[162] with little reference to the trinitarian shape of the incarnation and its relation to human being or to the Spirit, the importance of Irving's christology lies in the fact that his solution does not, as we have seen, involve a divorce from the classical doctrine of God as Trinity,[163] but rather a development of it in light of his understanding of both the incarnation and the nature of salvation. Indeed, Irving may be understood as complementing his christology by a 'search for the historical Spirit'.[164] Irving is clearly not guilty of Bobrinskoy's double criticism of traditional doctrines of the Spirit which on the one hand have reduced the doctrine of the Spirit 'to a single specific chapter of trinitarian theology' focusing either in the eternal procession of the Spirit from the Father, or from the Father and the Son, and on the other, limits 'its account of the function of the Spirit to a consideration of his gifts within the Church and his sanctifying activity in the spiritual life of the individual believers'.[165]

With Irving we meet a theology wherein 'the character of the Spirit has taken its "shape" from the impress of Jesus' own relationship with God'.[166] It involves an exploration of the 'interconnectedness' between the doctrines of Christ and the Spirit. Bobrinskoy identifies two fundamental question to this process which Irving articulates in detail. Firstly, there is the place of the Spirit in the redemptive work of the incarnate Son: in other words, the Spirit's place in the work of salvation. Secondly, there is the place of the Spirit within the eternal being of the Son and thus the conception of the Spirit's place in the very being of God.[167] Irving approaches both in a thoroughgoing dynamic manner. As Jüngel later argues, God may be expressed as a being which 'remains a being *which is coming*'.[168] This is not to suggest that God is

in any way incomplete or in the process of becoming
something more. Rather, God is dynamic. Through combining incarnational and inspirational themes, Irving establishes
a means of continuity between his understanding of the
affective and effective dynamics of salvation of the human
need of salvation and the divine gift of salvation. By means
of the place he gives the Spirit in the incarnation, Irving
'acknowledges that God's humanity as a story *which has
happened* does not cease being history *which is happening
now*', for the Spirit we receive in redemption is the same
Spirit who anointed, empowered and raised the God-man,
Jesus Christ.[169]

It is to Irving's credit that by the manner in which he has
developed his appreciation of the being of God and human
being, he has avoided two fundamental pitfalls. Firstly, he
has not minimized the work of the Spirit so that the Spirit is
relegated, at best, to an assumed but uninvolved place in
incarnation, and at worst, is completely ignored.[170] We see
this being worked out in many supposedly trinitarian interpretations of the incarnation which refer to the Spirit in
word only but offer little meaningful in terms of deed. And
as result, little thought, if any, is given to the status of the
Spirit in incarnation. This, by and large, was the context
within which Irving found himself: a context within which it
was difficult to articulate fully the Spirit's status in relation to
the incarnate Son; whether it be as Irving believed, both in
relation to the nature and character of the triune God, and
in relation to the saving work of God.

Secondly, Irving avoids the pitfall which Florovsky identifies as giving too much place to the humanity, where Christ
becomes the 'simple receptacle of the Spirit, thereby obscur-
ing the truth that the Savior is above all the "royal dwelling-
place", the living and unique *locus* of the full presence of the
Spirit, who belongs to him alone'.[171] As we have noted,
Irving's is no Spirit christology. The agent of incarnation is
not an inspired man; he is at all times the divine Son. Where
Irving advances our appreciation of the being of God in
incarnation, is in the manner by which he intimately identifies the Saviour with the object of salvation. In so doing, he
opens up a logical space which enables him to show that the

person and work of the Spirit in incarnation and in the being
of God, is 'that which realizes in the endless diversity of
human lives the set of renewed human possibilities opened
up by the work of Christ'.[172]

## Footnotes

[1] T Merton, *The Seven Storey Mountain*, London: Sheldon Press, 1975,
83.

[2] RF Thiemnan, *Revelation and Theology. The Gospel as Narrated
Promise*, Indiana: University of Notre Dame Press, 1985, 69.

[3] WA Andrews, 'Edward Irving: A Review', *The New Englander* July-
Oct 1863, Edinburgh: Thomas Laurie, 1864, 41–45.

[4] TV Morris, *The Logic Of God Incarnate*, Ithaca: Cornell University
Press, 1986, 64.

[5] G Kaufman, *Systematic Theology: A Historical Perspective*, New
York: Scribners, 1968, x.

[6] K Surin, *The Turnings of Darkness and Light. Essays in Philosophical
and Systematic Theology*, Cambridge: Cambridge University Press.
1989, 29.

[7] See CD Batson, *Commitment Without Ideology*, eds. CD Batson, JC
Baker, WM Clark, London: SCM Press Ltd, 1973, 25, TS Kuhn, *The
Structure of Scientific Revolutions*, Chicago: The University of Chi-
cago Press, 1962, 61–84ff., 109.

[8] See Surin, fn 39 Part I.

[9] See CE Gunton, *Yesterday and Today*, London: DLT, 1983; E
Krasevac, 'Christology from Above & Christology from Below', *The
Thomist*, 51, 1987, 299–306.

[10] This is perhaps a damning criticism when we consider that these two
doctrines undergird Irving's entire christology. PE Davies' 1928
Edinburgh thesis, *An Examination of the Views of Edward Irving
Concerning the Person and Work of Jesus Christ* assigns under 5 pages
to his anthropology. The aim of JJ Nantomah, in his 1982 Aberdeen
thesis, *Jesus the God-Man: the Doctrine of the Incarnation in Edward
Irving in the light of the Doctrine of the Church Fathers and its
relevance for a Twentieth century African Context* excludes any
detailed interaction with either doctrine. And whilst DD Dorries'
1987 Aberdeen thesis, *Nineteenth Century British Christological Controversy, Centring Upon Edward Irving's Doctrine of Christ's Human
Nature*, may be understood as an expansion of the former part of
Nantomah's less well-developed thesis, his argument, too, has little
recourse to developing independently Irving's doctrines of God and
man. CG Strachan, in the publication of his 1973 Edinburgh thesis,
*The Pentecostal Teaching of Edward Irving*, London: Darton, Longman & Todd, 1973, gives a more explicit presentation of Irving's

doctrine of God as Trinity, but here Strachan's interest lies with the
trinitarian understanding of the person and work of Christ in relation
to the Pentecostal doctrine of 'baptism with the Holy Spirit'. In
addition, little has been made of the individual and corporate relations
instituted by Christ and constituted by the Spirit except for K Ware,
*The Humanity of Christ. The Fourth Constantinople Lecture*, Anglican
and Eastern Churches Association, 1985, and CE Gunton, 'Two
Dogmas Revisited: Edward Irving's Christology', *Scottish Journal of
Theology*, 41.3, 1988, 359–376.

[11] AE McGrath, *The Making of Modern German Christology*, Oxford:
Basil Blackwell Ltd, 1986, 17–18.
[12] RR Williams, *Schleiermacher the Theologian. The Construction of the
Doctrine of God*, Philadelphia: Fortress Press, 1978, 143.
[13] FDE Schleiermacher, *The Christian Faith*, (ed.) trans. HR Mackintosh, JS Steward, Edinburgh: T&T Clark, 1986, §170.3, 741.
[14] CF, §170.1, 739.
[15] CF, §172, 747, italics author's.
[16] FDE Schleiermacher, 'On the Discrepancies between the Sabellian
and Athanasian Method of Representing the Doctrine of the Trinity,'
*The Biblical Repository and Quarterly Observer*, Andover: Gould and
Newman, No.XVIII, April 1835, 339–353, No.XIX, July 1835, 1–80,
52, italics author's.
[17] BRQO, XIX, 61.
[18] Lecture 13 (June 4, 1832), in KW Clements, *Friedrich Schleiermacher
Pioneer of Modern Theology*, London: Collins, 1987, 204–205.
[19] CF §89.3, 368.
[20] See CE Gunton, *The One, the Three and the Many*, Cambridge:
Cambridge University Press, 1993 for a penetrating analysis of this
thesis.
[21] CW5. 43, 77, 85.
[22] CW5, 56.
[23] CW5, 12. The theme of grace permeates Irving's entire theology.

> Sin . . . is a pre-requisite to grace; and only a sinner can be the subject
> of grace: others may know goodness; but sinners alone can know grace.
> Grace is not an attribute of God, like wisdom, power, holiness,
> justice, goodness, and truth: but a form of the will of God, where of all
> those are but the attributes or characteristics. As the will to create was
> waited on and carried into effect by all those attendant attributes, so
> also was the will to save. The act of grace is, therefore, like the act of
> creation, and hath its similitude in nothing else. It is another mood . . .
> in the Divine mind; another act in the great mystery of manifesting
> Himself. Grace, therefore, is not mercy, but mercy is to be seen in
> grace . . . and so of every other attribute of the Godhead. It is a new act
> of the Divine will, in which all the features of the Divinity will manifest
> themselves. CW5, 312, 315.

[24] CW5, 286.
[25] CW5, 30.

[26] CHF, vi. See Dorries, (Aberdeen 1987) for a clear and precise commentary on the orthodoxy of Irving's argument.

[27] CW5, 29–30.

[28] PW Pokornÿ, *The Genesis of Christology*, trans. M Lefébure, Edinburgh: T&T Clark, 1987, 61.

[29] PW1, 188–189.

[30] CW5, 422.

[31] GW Bromily, 'The Spirit of Christ', *Essays in Christology for Karl Barth*, London: Lutterworth Press, 1956, 133–152, 135.

[32] J Moltmann, 'The Unity of the Triune God', *St. Vladimir's Theological Quarterly*, 28.3, 1984, 157–171, 162.

[33] E McDonagh, 'The Holy Spirit and Human Identity', *The Irish Theological Quarterly*, 49.1, 1982, 37–49, 42.

[34] CD Batson, op cit, 125.

[35] J Meyendorff, 'Christ's Humanity: the Paschal Mystery', *St Vladimir's Theological Quarterly*, 31.1, 1987, 5–46, 24.

[36] VP Brannick, 'The Sinful Flesh of the Son of God (Rom.8:3): A Key Image of Pauline Theology', *The Catholic Biblical Quarterly*, 47, 1985, 246–262, 251. For a broader theological study of this subject, see H Johnson, *The Humanity of the Saviour*, London: The Epworth Press, 1962, or more recently, TG Weinandy, *In the Likeness of Sinful Flesh, An Essay on the Humanity of Christ*, Edinburgh: T&T Clark, 1993.

[37] K Ware, op cit, 4.

[38] CE Gunton, op cit. *SJT* 41.3, 366. Italics mine.

[39] J Meyendorff, op cit, 27. See also, W Pannenberg, *Jesus—God and Man*, London: SCM Press Ltd, 1986, 39: 'Almost all Christological conceptions have had soteriological motifs. Changes in the soteriological interest, in man's understanding of salvation, explain, at least in part, the different forms Christology has taken at different times.' P Tillich, *Systematic Theology Vol.2*, London: SCM Press Ltd, 1984, 150: 'Christology is a function of soteriology. The problem of soteriology creates the christological question and gives direction to the christological answer.' DM Baillie, *God was in Christ*, London: Faber and Faber Limited, 1973, 160, 'Throughout the Christian tradition the supreme human exigency to which the doctrine of the Incarnation had to be related and made relevant has been the need of salvation from sin, the forgiveness of sins.'

[40] SW Sykes, 'The Theology of the humanity of Christ', *Christ, Faith and History*, eds. SW Sykes and JP Clayton, Cambridge: Cambridge University Press, 1972, 53–71, 58–9. One who presents the tradition as it stands in stark contrast to Irving was Julian of Halicarnassus, who believed that Christ assumed an incorruptible, pre-fallen humanity which 'was not only sinless but . . . had no involvement in the fallen state of the human race', VC Samuel, 'One Incarnate Nature of God the Word', *The Greek Orthodox Theological Review*, Vol.X.2, 1964–65. Of interest here is the response given by JS Romanides discussing the unorthodox position taken by Julian:

The teaching of Julian of Halicarnassus that the Logos united to Himself manhood as it was before the fall is not in itself wrong and is accepted by all Fathers. What is wrong with Julian's position . . . is that the human nature of Christ was considered incorruptible before the resurrection. I would add that most Fathers would rather say that the human nature of Christ was by nature mortal but not by nature under the power of sentence of death and corruption which are the wages of sin . . . In this sense even angels are by nature mortal. Only God is by nature immortal. It is for this reason that the death of the Lord of Glory in the flesh was volunatry and not the wages of personal or inherited sin. (ibid. 52).

[41]  LHN, 4–5.
[42]  LHN, 6–7.
[43]  CW5, 244.
[44]  CW5, 244.
[45]  CW5, 3.
[46]  OCD, 50–51.
[47]  CW5, 115.
[48]  PW2, 464–465.
[49]  This is the central argument of Dorries' Aberdeen thesis: both that Irving's understanding of this term stands well within the perimeters of orthodoxy and that those who convicted him misunderstood his use of the term.
[50]  OCD, 27–28.
[51]  'Irving . . . took care, as Nestorius had done, to distinguish between the levels of *nature* and *person*, K Ware, op cit, 6–7. See also, Nantomah's thesis, 136–7 as well as E Brunner, *The Mediator. A Study of the Central Doctrine of the Christian Faith*, London: The Lutterworth Press, 1934, 319.
[52]  L Andrewes, *Ninety-Six Sermons by the Right Honourable and Reverend Father in God, Lancelot Andrewes, Sometime Lord Bishop of Winchester, in three volumes*. Vol.1, Oxford: John Henry Parker, 1891, 89.
[53]  CW5, 218.
[54]  CW5, 217.
[55]  CS, 14.
[56]  See K Barth, *Karl Barth's Table Talk*, ed. JD Godsey, *Scottish Journal of Theology Occassional Paters No 10*, Edinburgh: Oliver & Boyd, 68–69, where he argues:

Heinrich Vogel says that the human nature taken by Chist was a 'holy' flesh. I say no. It is *our* flesh, but if Christ takes on our flesh, then a sanctification of the flesh takes place, and then the man in Christ cannot sin. But the siꞏlessness of Christ is a deed, not a quality . . . *Non posse peccare* is a deed of God, not a quality . . . the quality of a sanctified life was *fight*, not just a being. Jesus had *to obey*. But it was a fight that could not have another result.

57 CW5, 174.

58 PW1, 105–106.

59 Brannick, op cit, 252.

60 *Letter of Thomas Erskine*, ed. H William, Edinburgh: David Douglas, 1877. Erskine writes about Christ:

> So he came into our flesh after it had fallen under the condemnation of death, and through his fulfillment of righteousness under these conditions he had overcome death and nullified the condemnation. 'Thoughts on St Paul's Epistle to the Romans', *The Spiritual Order & Other Papers*, Edinburgh: Edmonston & Douglas, 1871, 162–3.
>
> His assumption of our flesh in its actual conditions qualifies him in a special manner to act for us, (ibid, 164).

61 CE Gunton, *Yesterday and Today: A Study of Continuities in Christology*, London: Darton, Longman & Todd, 1983, 193.

62 CW5, 211.

63 CW5, 106.

64 CW5, 338.

65 CW5, 225.

66 CW5, 212.

67 CW5, 212.

68 CW5, 213.

69 CW5, 213–214.

70 CW5, 214.

71 CW5, 216.

72 CHF, 36.

73 OCD, 66–67.

74 J McIntyre, *The Shape of Christology*, London: SCM Press Ltd, 1966, 140.

75 *Shape*, 11.

76 D Bonhoeffer, *Lectures on Christology*, Glasgow: Collins, 1978, 30.

77 J Galot, *Who is Christ? A Theology of the Incarnation*, Rome: Gregorian University Press, 1980, 267.

78 W Kasper, *Jesus The Christ*, London: Burns and Oates, 1976, 20–24.

79 CW5, 438–439.

80 OCD, 29.

81 CW5, 124.

82 CHF, 5.

83 CW5, 159. There is a strong parallel here with Hooker's understanding of the 'person' of incarnation in, *The Works of Mr. Richard Hooker, In Eight Books of the Laws of Ecclesiastical Polity. In Three Volumes*, Vol.II, London: William Baynes and Son, 1822, 160–161.

> If the Son of God had taken to himself a man now made and already perfected, it would of necessity follow, that there are in Christ two persons, the one assuming, and the other assumed; whereas the Son of God did not assume a man's person into his own, but man's nature to

his own person and therefore took *semen*, the seed of Abraham, the very first original element of our nature, before it was come to have any personal human susbsistence. The flesh and the conjunction of the flesh with God, began both at the one instant; his making and taking to himself our flesh was but one act, so that in Christ there is no personal subsistence but one, and that from everlasting. By taking only the nature of man, he still continueth one person, and changeth but the manner of susbsisting, which was before in mere glory the Son of God, and is now in the habit of our flesh. Forasmuch . . . as Christ hath no personal subsistence but one, whereby we acknowledge him to have been eternally the Son of God, we must . . . apply to the person of the Son of God, even that example, according to the flesh he was born of the Virgin Mary, baptized by John in the river Jordan, by Pilate adjudged to die, and executed by the Jews. We cannot properly say, that the Virgin bore, or John did baptize, or Pilate condemn, or the Jews crucify, the nature of man, because there all are personable attributes; his person is the subject which receiveth them, his nature that which maketh his person capable . . . to receive. If we should say, that the person of a man in our Saviour Christ was the subject of these things, this were plainly to entrap ourselves in the very snare of the Nestorian heresy. The Son of God took not to himself a man's person, but the nature only of a man. Christ is a person both Divine and human, habit not therefore two persons in one; neither both these in one sense, but a person Divine, because he is personally the Son of God; human, because he hath really the nature of the children of man. In Christ, therefore, God and man, 'There is (saith Paschasius) a twofold substance, not a twofold person, because one person distinguisheth another, whereas one nature cannot in another become extinct'.

[84] P Schoonenberg, 'The Kenosis or Self-Emptying of Christ', *Concilium*, Vol.1.2, 1966, II, 27–36, 27.
[85] CW5, 405.
[86] L Richard, 'Kenotic Christology in a New Perspective', *Église et Théologie*, 7, 1976, 5–39, 27.
[87] J Macquarrie, 'Kenoticism Reconsidered', *Theology*, 77, 1974, 115–124, 122.
[88] CFD Moule, 'The Manhood of Jesus in the New Testament', *Christ, Faith and History. Cambridge Studies in Christology*, eds. SW Sykes, JP Clayton, Cambridge: Cambridge University Press, 1972, 95–110, 97.
[89] AT Hanson, *Grace and Truth*, London: SPCK, 1975, 22.
[90] Richard, op cit, 26.
[91] JAT Robinson, *The Human Face of God*, Philadelphia: Westminster Press, 1973, 208.
[92] K Barth, *Church Dogmatics* IV. 1, 211.
[93] PW1, 231. Also, CW5, 231.
[94] CW5, 280.
[95] CW5, 134.
[96] PW1, 14.

[97] See E Duffy, 'The Philosophers and the China Shop', *New Black-friars*, Oct.1988, 447–452, 499. In relation to the divinity and the person of Jesus Christ, Brunner states that 'Deity is the secret of this person', *The Mediator*, op cit. 347.

[98] CW5, 319.

[99] CW5, 160.

[100] Origen, *First Principles*, trans. GW Butterworth, II, London: Society for Promoting Christian Knowledge, 1936, ch.VI.3, 110.

[101] Origen, op cit, II.ch.VI.6, 113. Also, IV.ch.IV, 318–319.

[102] John of Damascus, *Exposition of the Christian Faith*, NPCF² Vol IX, Grand Rapids: Wm.B. Eerdmans Pulishing Company, 1983, 50.

[103] MF Wiles, 'The Nature of the Early Debate about Christ's Human Soul', *Journal of Ecclesiastical History*, XVI.2, 1965, 139–151, 141.

[104] Wiles, op cit, 148, and HA Wolfson, 'Philosophical Implications of Arianism and "Apollinarianism" ', *Dumbarton Oaks Papers*, Cambridge, Mass: Harvard University Press, 1958.

[105] *Letters*, Vol. III (131–164), trans. W Parsons, Washington D.C.: The Catholic University of America Press, 1965.

[106] Ambrose of Milan, *On the Sacrament of the Lord's Becoming Flesh*, 7, 65–68, cited in GH Ettlinger, *Jesus, Christ and Saviour*, Delaware: Michel Glazier, 1987, 144.

[107] Aquinas, *Summa Theologiæ*, Vol.48, 3a.1–6, London Blackfriars, 1976, 3a.6.a., 154.

[108] 3a.6.6., 173.

[109] This is a concern that is woven throughout *Christ in Christian Tradition*, Vol.1 2nd edn, A Grillmeier, trans. J Bowden, London: Mowbrays, 1975.

[110] CW5, 126.

[111] See G Lampe, *God as Spirit*, London: SCM Press Ltd, 1977 for such an approach. For a succinct appraisal of Lampe in relation to Irving, see CE Gunton, op cit, *SJT*, 41.3, 373–374.

[112] Cited in Grillmeier, op cit, 471.

[113] *Contra Arianos*, 1. 46, ET *Library of the Fathers*, Oxford, 1842, cited in NS Clark, 'Spirit Christology in the Light of Eucharistic Theology', *Heythrop Journal*, XXIII, 1982, 270–284, 271.

[114] CW5, 124.

[115] *The Works of John Owen*⁴, ed WH Goold, Vol.III, Edinburgh: The Banner of Truth Trust, 1981, 162–168. See A Spence, *Incarnation and Inspiriation: John Owen and the Coherence of Christology*, unpublished PhD, King's College, London, 1989. See also DW Bebbington, *Evangelicalism in Modern Britain. A History From the 1730s to the 1980s*, London: Unwin Hyman, 1989, 80.

[116] CW5, 94.

[117] B Hebblethwaite, *The Incarnation*, Cambridge: Cambridge University Press, 1987, 72, 161.

[118] LHN, 28–29.

[119] CW5, 433.

[120] W Wordsworth, 'The Excursion', Book Fourth, *The Poetical Works of William Wordsworth*, ed. W Knight, Edinburgh: William Paterson, 1884, 184.

[121] CW5, 121. Also, OCD, 32.

[122] MSS, British Library. See also DW Bebbington, op cit, 80–81.

[123] ST Coleridge, *Opus Maximum*, Toronto: Victoria University Library, Toronto, Canada, unpublished, 238–239.

[124] OM, 242.

[125] CHF, 63.

[126] OM, 242–243.

[127] *Aids*, 47.

[128] JD Boulger, *Coleridge as Religious Thinker*, New Haven: Yale University Press, 1961, 140.

[129] ST Coleridge, *Huntington MSS*, unpublished manuscript, San Marino, California: The Huntington Library, 39–43.

[130] OM, 119.

[131] See C Turk, *Coleridge and Mill*, Aldershot: Avebury, 1988, 157, and ST Coleridge, *Aids to Reflection*[7], London: Edward Moxon, 1854, 119, respectively.

[132] OM, 119.

[133] OM, 230.

[134] SLOD, 24.

[135] Coleridge, *Aids*, 217, Irving, CHF, 3–5. See also O Pfleidderer, *The Development of Theology in Germany since Kant and its Progress in Great Britain since 1825*, London: Swan Sonnenschein and Co., 1890, 310, where Pfleidderer points out that Coleridge's understanding of original sin is much more a Kantian than biblical one.

[136] OCD, 66–67.

[137] See T Erskine, *The Unconditional Freeness of the Gospel*, 1828, *An Essay on Faith*, Edinburgh: Waugh and Innes, 1829, *The Purpose of God in the Creation of Man*, Edinburgh: Edmonston & Douglas, 1870. See also TA Hart, *Thomas Erskine*, The Devotional Library, Edinburgh: Saint Andrew Press, 1993.

[138] CHF, 14. Note the strong parallel here with Theodore of Mopsuestia, *Commentary of Theodore of Mopsuestia on the Nicene Creed*, Woodbrooke Studies, Vol.V, Cambridge, Mass: W Heffer & Sons Limited, 1932, 56–57.

> It was necessary that He should assume not only the body but also the immortal and rational soul; and not only the death of the body had to cease but also that of the soul, which is sin . . . It was . . . necessary that sin should have first been abolished, as after its abolition there would be no entry for death. It is indeed clear that the strength of sin has its origin in the will of the soul . . . It was . . . necessary that Christ should assume not only the body but also the soul . . . The enemy of the soul had to be removed first and then for the sake of it that of the body, because if death is from sin and the same death is in the corruption of the body, sin would have first to be abolished and the abolition of death would follow by itself.

139 CHF 14.
140 DM MacKinnon, 'Prologomena to Christology', *The Journal of Theological Studies*, XXXIII.1, 1982, 146–160, 157.
141 CW4, 482.
142 CW4, 271.
143 OCD, 23.
144 PW2, 209.
145 EL Mascall, *Christ, The Christian and the Church*, London: Longmans, Green and Co., 1946, 36.
146 CW5, 166, also, 134.
147 PW1, 387.
148 CW5, 439, also, 320–321; CHF, 9.
149 CW5, 529.
150 CW5, 134, 437.
151 S Kierkegaard, *Journals and Papers*, eds. trans. HV Hong, EM Hong, Vol.2, Bloomington: Indiana University Press, 1962, 137.
152 2 Timothy 2:5.
153 LHN, 66–67.
154 CS, 25.
155 E Brunner, *The Mediator*, op cit, 493.
156 TM, 493.
157 H Johnson, *The Humanity of the Saviour*, op cit, 155.
158 PW1, 12–13.
159 Strachan, op cit, 22.
160 E Schweizer, *The Holy Spirit*, London: SCM Press Ltd, 1981, 48.
161 N Hook, 'A Spirit Christology', *Theology*, 75, 1972, 226–232, 226.
162 D Ritschl, *The Logic of Theology*, London: SCM Press Ltd, 1986.
163 T Dunn, 'Trinity and History', *Theological Studies*, 45, 1984, 139–152, 143.
164 T Dunn, ibid.
165 B Bobrinskoy, 'The Indwelling of the Spirit in Christ. "Pneumatic Christology" in the Cappadocian Fathers', *St. Vladimir's Theological Quarterly*, 28.1, 1984, 49–65, 49.
166 JDG Dunn, *Jesus and the Spirit*, London: SCM Press Ltd, 1975, 320.
167 Bobrinskoy, op cit, 49.
168 E Jüngel, *God as the Mystery of the World*, Edinburgh: T&T Clark Ltd, 1983, 304.
169 Jüngel, op cit, 304.
170 A recent example of this is TF Torrance who advocates a return to an Athanasian interpretation of divine being, but has not addressed the deficiency of Athanasius' doctrine of the Spirit. TF Torrance, *The Trinitarian Faith*, Edinburgh: T&T Clark, 1988.
171 Cited in Bobrinskoy, op cit, 61.
172 V Lossky, *The Mystical Theology of the Eastern Church*, London, 1957, 166–167.

# Bibliography—By Edward Irving

*Babylon and Infidelity foredoomed of God: A Discourse on the Prophecies of Daniel and the Apocalypse which relate to these latter times, and until the Second Advent*, Second Edition, Glasgow: William Collins, 1828.

*Christ's Holiness in the Flesh, the Form, Fountain Head, and Assurance to us of Holiness in the Flesh. In Three Parts*, Edinburgh: John Lindsay and Co., 1831.

*The Church and State Responsible to Christ, and to One Another. A Series of Discourses on Daniel's Vision of the Four Beasts*, London: James Nisbet, 1829.

*The Collected Writings of Edward Irving in Five Volumes*, ed. Rev. G. Carlyle, London: Alexander Strahan, 1864.

*The Confession of Faith and the Books of Discipline on the Church of Scotland, of date Anterior to the Westminster Confession*, London: Baldwin and Craddock, 1831.

*The Day of Pentecost or the Baptism with the Holy Ghost*, Edinburgh: John Lindsay, 1830.

*The Doctrine Held by the Church of Scotland Concerning the Human Nature of Our Lord, As Stated in Her Standards*, Edinburgh: John Lindsay.

*Exposition of the Book of Revelation in a series of lectures, In four Volumes*, London: Baldwin and Craddock, 1831.

*Farewell Discourse to the Congregation and Parish of St. John's, Glasgow*, Glasgow: Waugh and Innes, 1822.

*For the Oracles of God, Four Orations and for the Judgement to Come, An Argument in Nine Parts*, London: T. Hamilton, 1824.

*The Last Days: A Discourse on the Evil Character of These our Times: Proving Them to be the 'Perilous Times' of the 'Last Days'*, London: RB Sulley and W Burnside, 1828.

'On the Human Nature of Christ', *The Morning Watch, Vol.I*, 1829.

'On the True Humanity of Christ', *The Morning Watch, Vol.II*, 1829.

*The Opinions Circulating Concerning Our Lord's Human Nature*, Edinburgh: John Lindsay, 1830.

*The Orthodox and Catholic Doctrine of Our Lord's Human Nature, Tried by the Westminster Confession of Faith. Set in Four parts*, London: Baldwin and Craddock, 1830.

*A Pastoral Letter From the Scottish Presbytery in London Addressed To the Baptized of the Scottish Church Residing in London and its Vicinity and in the Southern Parts of the Island*, London: James Nisbet, 1828.

*Preliminary Discourse to the work of Ben Ezra: Entitled the Coming of Messiah in Glory and Majesty*, London: Bosworth and Harrison, 1859.

*The Prophetical Works of Edward Irving in Two Volumes*, ed. Rev. G Carlyle. London: Alexander Strahan, 1865.

*Sermons and Exposition*, London: W Harding, 1833.

*Sermons, Lectures and Occasional Discourses in Three Volumes*, London: RB Sulley and W Burnside, 1828.

'The Signs of the Times:', *Irving's Tracts*, London: Andrew Panton, 1829.

## Abbreviations

CHF    *Christ's Holiness in the Flesh, the Form, Fountain Head, and Assurance to us of Holiness in the Flesh. In Three Parts*, Edinburgh: John Lindsay and Co., 1831.

CW    *The Collected Writings of Edward Irving in Five Volumes*, ed. Rev. G. Carlyle, London: Alexander Strahan, 1864.

CS    *The Doctrine Held by the Church of Scotland Concerning the Human Nature of Our Lord, As Stated in Her Standards*, Edinburgh: John Lindsay.

OG    *For the Oracles of God, Four Orations and for the Judgement to Come, An Argument in Nine Parts*, London: T. Hamilton, 1824.

LD      *The Last Days: A Discourse on the Evil Character of These our Times: Proving Them to be the 'Perilous Times' of the 'Last Days'*, London: RB Sulley and W Burnside, 1828.

MW      *The Morning Watch*, Vol.V, VII, 1833.

OCD     *The Orthodox and Catholic Doctrine of Our Lord's Human Nature, Tried by the Westminster Confession of Faith. Set in Four parts*, London: Baldwin and Craddock, 1830.

PW      *The Prophetical Works of Edward Irving in Two Volumes*, ed. Rev. G Carlyle. London: Alexander Strahan, 1865.

# Bibliography of Contents

Alsford SE, *Sin as a Problem of Twentieth Century Systematic Theology*, unpublished PhD Thesis, University of Durham, 1987.

Ambrose, *On the Sacrament of the Lord's Becoming Flesh*, 7, 65–68. in GH Ettlinger, *Jesus, Christ and Saviour*, Delaware: Michel Glazier, 1987.

Anastos MV, 'Basil's Κατα Ευνομιου, A Critical Analysis', *Basil of Caeserea: Christian, Humanist, Ascetic. Part One*, ed. PJ Fenwick, Toronto: Pontifical Institute of Mediaeval Studies, 1981, 67–136.

Andrewes L, *Ninety-Six Sermons by the Right Honourable and Reverend Father in God, Lancelot Andrewes, Sometime Lord Bishop of Winchester*, In 3 Volumes, Oxford: John Henry Parker, 1891.

Andrews WA, 'Edward Irving: A Review', *New Englander*, (July-Oct 1863), Edinburgh: Thomas Laurie, 1864, 41–45.

Aquinas T, *Summa Theologiae*, Vol.48, 3a.1–6, London: Blackfriars, 1976.

Athanasius, *The Incarnation of the Word of God*, London: Geoffrey Bles, The Centenery Press, 1944.

Augustine, *The Trinity*, Washington DC: The Catholic University of America Press, 1981, 3rd edn.

Baillie DM, *God was in Christ*, London: Faber and Faber Limited, 1973.

Barth K, *Church Dogmatics*, Edinburgh: T&T Clark, 1980.

—— *Karl Barth's Table Talk*, ed. JD Godsey, *Scottish Journal of Theology Occassional Papers No.10*, Edinburgh: Oliver & Boyd, 1963.

—— *The Knowledge of God and the service of God according to the teaching of the Reformation*, London: Hodder and Stoughton Publishers, 1949.

Basil of Caeserea, *Letters*, Nicene and Post-Nicene Fathers, Second Series, Michigan: Wm. B Eerdmans Publishing Co., 1978, Vol.VIII.

—— *De Spirito Sanctu*, Nicene and Post-Nicene Fathers, Second Series, Michigan: Wm. B Eerdmans Publishing Co., 1978, Vol.VIII.

Batson CD, *Commitment Without Ideology*, eds. CD Batson, JC Baker, WM Clark, London: SCM Press Ltd, 1973.

Bebbington DW, *Evangelicalism in Modern Britain. A History From the 1730s to the 1980s*, London: Unwin Hyman, 1989.

Bobrinskoy B, 'The Indwelling of the Spirit in Christ. "Pneumatic Christology" in the Cappadocian Fathers', *St Vladimir's Theological Quarterly*, 28.1, 1984, 49–65.

Bonhoeffer D, *Lectures on Christology*, Glasgow: Collins, 1961.

Boulger JM, *Coleridge as Religious Thinker*, New Haven: Yale Unversity Press, 1961.

Brannick VP, 'The Sinful Flesh of the Son of God (Rom 8:3): A Key Image of Pauline Theology', *The Catholic Biblical Quarterly*, 47, 1985, 246–262.

Bromily GW, 'The Spirit of Christ', *Essays in Christology for Karl Barth*, London: Lutterworth Press, 1956, 133–152.

Brunner E, *The Mediator. A Study on the Central Teaching of the Christian Faith*, London: The Lutterworth Press, 1934.

Calvin J, *Institutes of the Christian Religion*, Philadelphia: The Westminster Press, 1960.

Campbell JM, *The Nature of the Atonement*, London: James Clark and Co. Ltd., 1949.

Carroll L, *Alice's Adventures in Wonderland, and Through the Looking Glass*, London: JM Dent & Sons Ltd, 1981.

Clark NS, 'Spirit Christology in the Light of Eucharistic Theology', *The Heythrop Journal*, XXIII, 1982, 270–284.

Clements KW, *Friedrich Schleiermacher. Pioneer of Modern Theology*, London: Collins, 1987.

Coleridge ST, *Aids to Reflection*, 7th edn. London: Edward Moxon, 1854.

—— *The Complete Works of Samuel Taylor Coleridge. In 7 volumes*, New York: Harper & Brothers.

—— *Huntington MSS*, unpublished. The Huntington Library, San Marino, California.

—— *Literary Remains*, vol.3, London: William Pickering, 1883.

—— *Opus Maximum*, Toronto: Victoria University Library, Toronto, Canada, unpublished.

—— *Unpublished Letters of Samuel Taylor Coleridge*, ed. EL Griggs, London: Constable & Co Ltd, 1932.

Cullmann O, *The Christology of the New Testament*, London: SCM Press Ltd, 1959.

Cupitt D, *After All*, London: SCM Press Ltd, 1994.

Davies PE, *An Examination of the Views of Edward Irving Concerning the Person and Work of Jesus Christ*, unpublished PhD thesis, Edinburgh, 1928.

Dickenson E, *Collected Poems*, New York: Routledge, 1982.

Dorries DD, *Nineteenth Century British Christological Controversy, Centring Upon Edward Irving's Doctrine of Christ's Human Nature*, unpublished PhD thesis, Edinburgh, 1987.

Duffy E, 'The Philosophers and the China Shop', *Blackfriars*, Oct. 1988.

Dunn JDG, *Jesus and the Spirit*, London: SCM Press Ltd, 1975.

Dunne T, 'Trinity and History', *Theological Studies*, 45, 1984, 139–152.

El-Khoury N, 'Anthropological Concepts in the School of Antioch', *Studia Patristica*, XVII, Part II, ed. EA Livingstone, Oxford: Pergamon Press, 1982, 1359–1365.

Erskine T, *An Essay on Faith*, Edinburgh: Waugh and Innes, 1829.

—— *Letters of Thomas Erskine*, ed. Hanna Williams, Edinburgh: David Douglas, 1877.

—— *The Purpose of God in the Creation of Man*, Edinburgh: Edmonston & Douglas, 1870.

—— *The Unconditional Freeness of the Gospel*, Edinburgh: Waugh & Innes, 1828.

—— 'Thoughts on St Paul's Epistle to the Romans', *The Spiritual Order & Other Papers*, Edinburgh: Edmonston & Douglas, 1871.

Frost R, *The Poetry of Robert Frost*, London: Jonathan Cape, 1976.

Gadamer HG, *Truth and Method*, London: Sheed & Ward, 1975.

Gervase M, 'Byzantine Aesthetics', in AM Allchin, *Sacrament & Image*, Fellowship of St Alban & St Sergius, 1987.

Gregory of Nazianzus, *The Theological Orations*, Michigan: Wm. B Eerdmans Publishing Co., 1978.

Gregory of Nyssa, *On Not Three Gods*, Christology of the Later Fathers, vol.III, Philadelphia: Westminster Press, MCMLIV.

Grillmeier A, *Christ in Christian Tradition*, Vol.1, London: Mowbrays, 1975.

Gunton CE, *Christ and Creation*, Carlisle: The Paternoster Press, 1992.

—— *The One, the Three and the Many*, Cambridge: Cambridge University Press, 1993.

—— *The Transcendent Lord. The Spirit and the Church in Calvanist and Cappadocian*, London: Reprocopy, 1988.

—— 'Two Dogmas Revistited: Edward Irving's Christology', *Scottish Journal of Theology*, 41.3, 1988, 359–376.

—— *Yesterday and Today: A Study of Continuities in Christology*, London: Darton, Longman & Todd, 1983.

Hall DJ, *Imaging God: Dominion as Stewardship*, Grand Rapids: Wm B Eerdmans Publishing Co., 1986.

Hanson A, *Grace and Truth*, London: SPCK, 1975.

Hanson RPC, *The Making of the Doctrine of the Trinity*, Anglican and Eastern Churches Association, 1984.

Hardy DW, 'Coleridge on the Trinity', *The Anglican Theological Review*, LXIX:2, 1988, 145–155.

Hardy ER, *Christology of the Later Fathers*, Philadelphia: The Westminster Press, 1954.

Harnack A, *History of Dogma*, vol.VII, London: Williams & Norgate, 1899.

Hebblethwaite B, *The Incarnation*, Cambridge: Cambridge University Press, 1987.

Heidegger M, *Being and Time*, London: SCM Press Ltd, 1962.

Hesse H, *Strange News from Another Star and Other Tales*, New York: Farrar, Strava & Groux, 1972.

Hook N, 'A Spirit Christology', *Theology*, 75, 1972, 276–232.

Hooker R, *The Works of Mr. Richard Hooker, In Eight Books of the Laws of Ecclesiastical Polity. In Three Volumes*. London: William Baynes and Son, 1822.

Irenaeus, *Against Heresies*, Ante-Nicene Christian Library, vol.V, Edinburgh: T&T Clark, 1880.

John of Damascus, *Exposition of the Christian Faith*, Nicene and Post-Nicene Fathers, Second Series, vol.IX, Grand Rapids: Wm B Eerdmans Publishing Co., 1983.

Johnson EA, 'Christology's Impact on the Doctrine of God', *Heythrop Journal*, XXVI, 1985, 143–163.

Johnson H, *The Humanity of the Saviour*, London: Epworth Press, 1962.

E Jüngel, *The Doctrine of the Trinity*, Edinburgh: Scottish Academic Press, 1976.

Kasper W, *Jesus the Christ*, London: Burn and Oates, 1976.

—— *The God of Jesus Christ*, London: SCM Press Ltd, 1984.

Kaufman GD, *An Essay on Theological Method*, Missoula: Scholars Press, 1979.

—— *Systematic Theology: A Historical Perpsective*, New York: Scribner's, 1986.

Keisling C, 'On Relating to the Persons of the Trinity', *Theological Studies*, 47, 1986, 599–616.

Kelly JND, *Early Christian Doctrines*, London: Adam & Charles Black, 1977.

Kelsey DH, *Christian Theology*, eds. P Hodgson, R King, London: SPCK, 1983.

Kierkegaard S, *Journals and Papers*, eds. HV Hong, EM Hong, vol.2, Bloomington: Indiana University Press, 1962.

Krasevac E, 'Christology from Above & Christology from Below', *The Thomist*, 1987, 299–306.

Kuhn TS, *The Structure of Scientific Revolutions*, Chicago: The University of Chicago Press, 1962.

LaCugna CM, *God For Us*, San Fransisco: Harper Collins, 1991.

Lampe G, *God as Spirit*, London: SCM Press Ltd, 1983.

Lewis CS, *God in the Dock*, Glasgow: William Collins' Sons & Co Ltd, 1979.

Lossky V, *The Mystical Theology of the Eastern Church*, New York: St. Vladimir's Seminary Press, 1976.

Luther M, *Commentary on Genesis*, Saint Louis: Conccordia Publishing House, 1958.

Marshall B, *Christology in Conflict*, Oxford: Basil Blackwell, 1987.

Martland TR, 'A Study of Cappadocian and Augustinian Trinitarian Methodology', *Anglican Theological Review*, 47, 1965, 252–263.

Mascall EL, *The Triune God. An Ecumenical Study*, Worthing: Churchman Publishing Ltd., 1986.

Maus M, 'A Category of the Human Mind', *Category of the Person*, eds. M Carrithers, S Collins, S Lukes, Cambridge: Cambridge University Press, 1988.

Merton T, *The Seven Storey Mountain*, London: Sheldon Press, 1975.

Meyendorff J, 'Christ's Humanity: the Paschal Mystery', *St. Vladimir's Theological Quarterly*, 31.1, 1987, 5–46.

Moltmann J, 'The Unity of the Triune God', *St. Vladimir's Theological Quarterly*, 28.3, 1984, 157–171.

Morris TV, *The Logic of God Incarnate*, Ithaca: Cornell University Press, 1986.

Moule CFD, 'The Manhood of Jesus in the New Testament', *Christ, Faith and History. Cambridge Studies in Christology*. eds. SW Sykes, JP Clayton, Cambridge: Cambridge University Press, 1972, 95–110.

Mozley JK, 'Christology and Soteriology', *Mysterium Christi. Christological Studies by British and German Theologians*, eds. GKA Bell, A Deissmann, London: Longmans, Green and Co., 1930.

McDonagh E, 'The Holy Spirit and Human Identity', *The Irish Theological Quarterly*, 49.1, 1982, 37–49.

McFadyen AI, *The Call to Personhood*, Cambridge: Cambridge University Press, 1990.

McGrath AE, *The Making of Modern German Christology*, Oxford: Basil Blackwell Ltd, 1986.

McGraw JG, 'God and the Problem of Loneliness', *Religious Studies*, 28, 1993, 319–346.

MacIntyre J, *The Shape of Christology*, London: SCM Press Ltd., 1966.

Mackey JP, *The Christian Experience of God as Trinity*, London: SCM Press Ltd., 1983.

MacKinnon DM, 'Prolegomena to Christology', *The Journal of Theological Studies*, XXXIII.1, 1982, 146–160.

Macquarrie J, 'Kenoticism Reconsidered', *Theology*, 77, 1974, 115–124.

Nantomah JJ, *Jesus the God-Man the Doctrine of the Incarnation in Edward Irving in the light of the Teaching of the Church Fathers and its relevance for a Twentieth century African context*, unpublished PhD, Aberdeen, 1982.

Newman PW, *A Spirit Christology*, Lanham: University Press of America, 1987.

Oliphant MOW, *Edward Irving*, London: Hurst and Blackett, 5th ed, no date.

Origen, *First Principles*, London: Society for Promoting Christian Knowledge, 1936.

Otis B, 'Cappadocian Thought as a Coherent System', *Dumbarton Oaks Papers*, 12, Mass: Harvard University Press, 1958, 95–124.

Owen J, *The Works of John Owen*, vol.III, Edinburgh: The Banner of Truth Trust, 1982.

O'Donnell J, 'The Trinity as Divine Community', *Gregorianum*, 69.1, 1988, 5–34.

Pannenberg W, *Jesus—God and Man*, Philadelphia: The Westminster Press, 1968.

Pelikan J, *The Emergence of the Catholic Tradition (100–600)*, Chicago: The University of Chicago Press, 1972.

Pfleidderer O, *The Development of Theology In Germany since Kant and its Progress in Great Britain since 1825*, London: Swan Sonnenschein and Co., 1890.

202    *Christ and the Spirit*

Pokorny P, *The Genesis of Christology*, Edinburgh: T&T Clark, 1987.

Polanyi M, *Personal Knowledge. Towards a Post-Critical Philosophy*, London: Routledge & Kegam Paul, 1987.

Prestige KR, *God in Patristic Thought*, London: SPCK, 5th ed. 1985.

Pruch B, *Basile de Césarèe sur le Saint-Esprit*, Sources Chrétiennes, 17bis.

Rahner K, *The Trinity*, New York: Herder and Herder, 1970.

Richard L, 'Kenotic Christology in a New Perspective', *Église et Théologie*, 7, 1976, 5–39.

Richard of St Victor, 'Book 3 of the Trinity', London: SPCK, 1979, trans. GA Zinn, *Benjamin Minor*, West Germany: Wiedfeld & Mehl, 1960, trans. SV Yanowski.

Ritschl D, *The Logic of Theology*, London: SCM Press Ltd, 1986.

Robinson JAT, *The Human Face of God*, Philadelphia: Westminster Press, 1973.

Samuel VC, 'One Incarnate Nature of God the Word', *The Greek Orthodox Theological Review*, vol.X.2, 1964–1965.

Schleiermacher FD, *The Christian Faith*, Edinburgh: T&T Clark, 1986.

—— 'On the Discrepancies between the Sabellian and Athanasian Method of Representing the Doctrine of the Trinity', *The Biblical Repository and Quarterly Observer*, XVIII, April 1835, 339–353, XIX, July, 1835, 1–80, Andover: Gould and Newman, 1835.

Schœnberg A, *Moses und Aron*, Uxbridge: The Hillingdon Press, 1974.

Schoonenberg P, 'The Kenosis or Self-Emptying of Christ', *Concilium*, 1966 II, vol.2, 27–36.

Schweitzer E, *The Holy Spirit*, London: SCM Press Ltd, 1981.

Sophrony, *The Monk of Mount Athos*, London: Mowbrays, 1973.

Spence A, *Incarnation and Inspiration: John Owen and the Coherence of Christology*, unpublished PhD thesis, King's College (KQC), The University of London, 1989.

Strachan CG, *The Pentecostal Theology of Edward Irving*, London: Darton, Longman & Todd, 1973.

Surin K, *The Turnings of Darkness and Light. Essays in Philosophical and Systematic Theology*, Cambridge: Cambridge University Press, 1989.

Sykes SW, 'The Theology of the humanity of Christ', *Christ, Faith and History. Cambridge Studies in Christology*, eds. SW Sykes, JP Clayton, Cambridge: Cambridge University Press, 1972, 53–71.

Tertullian, *On the Flesh of Christ*, The Ante-Nicene Fathers, vol.III, Buffalo: The Christian Literature Publishing Co, 1885.

TeSelle E, *Christ in Conflict. Divine Purpose & Human Possibility*, Philadelphia: Fortress Press, 1975.

Thiemann RF, *Revelation and Theology. The Gospel as Narrated Promise*, Indiana: University of Notre Dame Press, 1985.

Theodore of Mopsuestia, *Commentary of Theodore of Mosuestia on the Nicene Creed*, Woodbrooke Studies, vol.V, Cambridge, Mass: W Heffer & Sons Limited, 1932.

Tillich P, *Systematic Theology*, vol.2, Chichago: University of Chicago Press, 1957.

Torrance TF, *Calvin's Doctrine of Man*, London: Lutterworth Press, 1952.

—— 'The Goodness and Dignity of Man in the Christian Tradition', *Modern Theology*, 4.4, 1988, 309–322.

Turk C, *Coleridge and Mill*, Aldershot: Avebury, 1988.

Verheyden JC, *The Life of Schleiermacher*, Philadelphia: Fortress Press, 1975.

Ware K, *The Humanity of Christ. The Fourth Constantinople Lecture*, Anglican and Eastern Churches Association, 1985.

—— 'The Unity of Human Persons According to the Greek Fathers', *Persons and Personality. A Contemporary Inquiry*, eds. A Peacocke, G Gillett, Oxford: Basil Blackwell Ltd., 1987, 197–206.

Weinandy TG, *In the Likeness of Sinful Flesh*, Edinburgh: T&T Clark, 1993.

Wendebourg D, 'From the Cappadocian Fathers to Gregory Palamas. The Defeat of Trinitarian Theology', *Studia Patristica*, vol.XVII: Part 1, ed. EA Livingstone, Oxford: Pergamon Press, 1982, 194–198.

Westermann C, *Creation*, Philadelphia: Fortress Press, 1974.

Wiles MF, 'The Nature of the Early Debate about Christ's Human Soul', *Journal of Ecclesiastical History*, XVI.2, 1965, 139–151.

Williams RR, *Schleiermacher the Theologian. The Construction of the Doctrine of God*, Philadelphia: Fortress Press, 1978.

Wolfson HA, 'Philisophical Implications of Arianism and Apollinarianism', *Dumbarton Oaks Papers*, 12, Cambridge Mass: Harvard University Press, 1958.

—— *The Philosophy of the Church Fathers. Faith, Trinity, Incarnation*, third edition, Cambridge, Mass: Harvard University Press, 1976.

Wolfe T, *Of Time and the River. A Legend of Man's Hunger in His Youth*, New York: Charles Scribner's Sons, 1952.

Wordsworth W, *The Poetical Works of William Wordsworth*, ed. W Knight, Edinburgh: William Paterson.

Yu CT, *Being and Relation. A Theological Critique of Western Dualism and Individualism*, Edinburgh: Scottish Academic Press, 1987.

Zizioulas JN, *Being as Communion*, London: Darton, Longman and Todd Ltd., 1985.

—— *Credo in Spiritum Sanctum*, Rome: Vaticana Libreria Editrice, no date, 29–54.